WILD FLOWERS

of

North Carolina

Published with the

Sponsorship of

The Garden Club of North Carolina

and

The North Carolina Botanical Garden

Venus' Fly Trap Dionaea muscipula

The University of
North Carolina Press
Chapel Hill

WILD FLOWERS *of* *North Carolina*

William S. Justice

and

C. Ritchie Bell

Manufactured in the United States of America
ISBN 0-8078-1064-9
ISBN 0-8078-4192-7 (pbk.)
Library of Congress Catalog Card Number 68-18051

04 03 02 01 00 17 16 15 14 13

Acknowledgments

The authors owe many thanks to all those who have made the associations involved in the preparation of this book so pleasant and enjoyable. We wish to thank especially Dr. John Barber for his encouragement and his friendly companionship on numerous photographic field trips; Mr. Gladstone McDowell for his help in locating some of the rarer specimens; Mrs. John DuBose and Mr. and Mrs. Thomas Shinn for their contagious enthusiasm for, and interest in, our wild flowers and for making their excellent material available for study and photographing. The authors greatly appreciate the careful and critical review of the manuscript by Mrs. Ruth Landolina and Dr. Robert L. Wilbur and the many helpful suggestions made by Dr. A. E. Radford. Grateful acknowledgment is made to the New York Botanical Garden for permission to reprint a number of color slides that are included in this volume.

Not only the authors, but all who find this book helpful or enjoyable, owe continuing thanks to all of the members of the Garden Club of North Carolina whose foresight, interest, and efforts made a publication of this scope possible.

Contents

Introduction

The beauty and abundance of the native flowers of eastern America was impressive even to the earliest explorers and colonists, and the early reports and letters sent back to Europe often made reference to the variety of plants in the New World and to their uses. Although land was cleared for crops, trees were cut for fuel and shelter, and many plants were gathered by the settlers for food, medicine, and dye, with such vast lands and so few inhabitants, there was probably little change in the native flora for more than two centuries after colonization began. At first, neither the few European weeds that were doubtless established at an early date in the fields of the coastal farms and plantations nor the few plants intentionally introduced for horticultural or agricultural purposes that escaped and became naturalized, posed any threat to the established native plants. During the past century, however, the tremendous increase in the population and the more rapid and extensive clearing of the forests and other changes of the surface of the earth by man has had a profound effect on our native vegetation. This is especially true in the case of many of the more showy species collectively known as "Wild Flowers." Because of their delicately balanced adaptation to very specific natural environments, many wild flowers cannot grow in habitats that have been altered or disturbed, nor can they compete with the plants of the more weedy introduced species that rapidly invade the vast areas of land opened or altered by the machines of man for roads, farms, dwellings, and industrial complexes. Each year a few new plants are either intentionally or unintentionally introduced into our flora. In this changing balance of nature, some native species of plants, once relatively frequent, are now quite rare, and some introduced species, once rare, are now widespread and common. Thus the balance continues to shift so that today many of our most attractive native plants are near extinction except within the boundaries of the parks, natural areas, and gardens set aside for the preservation of interesting natural habitats and their associated plant and animal species.

An attempt to preserve rare or threatened species has led to the establishment of several natural gardens in North Carolina. In these gardens, plants rescued from the path of the bulldozer can be maintained in an approximation of their natural habitat for both scientific study and for the enjoyment of interested visitors. In the western part of the state are the Daniel Boone Native Garden at Boone and the Asheville-Biltmore Botanical Garden at Asheville, near the center of the state is the North Carolina Botanical Garden at Chapel Hill, and along the coast south of Wilmington is the Brunswick Town Nature Trail.

With the increasing elimination of the highly specialized habitats that account for the variety of our flora, establishment of small public natural gardens in each section of the state is essential to the preservation of many of our rarer species. As resources increase, it is hoped that, in addition to the array of special habitats already present in the North Carolina Botanical Garden, such other conditions may be developed as are required for the growth and display of most of the four hundred flowers illustrated in this book.

If given adequate light, water, and soil conditions, many of the native plants that once formed the "Natural Gardens of North Carolina" are equally as colorful and interesting, or even more so, than related horticultural varieties. The purpose of this book is to make easier the recognition of some of these flowers and thereby to stimulate a greater interest in this beautiful natural resource and accent the need for its preservation.

FORMAT

In the limited space available for the text material associated with each of the four hundred plants illustrated, an attempt has been made to cover the following specific items of information that are most useful to the person interested in the flowering plants of North Carolina and the surrounding regions:

1. Common name
2. Scientific name
3. Whether the plant is native or introduced
4. Plant or flower size
5. General comments on interesting botanical or other aspects of the plant

6. Frequency, especially if very rare or very common
7. Habitat
8. Range in North Carolina
9. General range in the U.S.
10. Months in bloom in our area
11. Index number.

Since each of the brief entries is independent of the others, and since each entry can be read in only a few seconds, the information concerning items 3-9 will not always be in the exact sequence given above, but may vary as seems appropriate for easy reading. Comments concerning the application of each bit of information are given, by category, in the following paragraphs.

Common name

If a native plant of North America had any resemblance to one in Europe, the early colonists applied the European common name to the new world plant even though the two were completely unrelated botanically. Depending upon the country or area of origin of the colonists, one particular plant might have several common names in different parts of this country. Or a given plant might have two or more common names in a single area because of different aspects of its appearance or use: thus the attraction of the colorful flowers of *Asclepias tuberosa* for butterflies accounts for the common name "Butterfly Weed" while an old medicinal use accounts for the common name "Pleurisy-root." On the other hand, a single name might be applied to a number of different plants: the common name "Buttercup," for example, has been given to plants belonging to several of the yellow-flowered species of *Ranunculus* (in the family Ranunculaceae) and also to several species of the completely unrelated genus *Narcissus* (in the family Amaryllidaceae). Common names are sometimes easier to remember than the scientific name but they are certainly not exact! Furthermore, many common names are the same as the generic name or the first part of the scientific name, such as Rhododendron, Iris, Trillium, Magnolia, Sassafras, and Oxalis, and no one ever thinks of these names as being too hard to learn.

Scientific name

The scientific name of a plant consists of two Latin or latinized words, a genus or *generic* name followed by a species name or *specific epithet*. By international agreement on the rules governing the formation of scientific names of plants, no two kinds may have the same name; thus every kind of plant has a different combination of generic name and specific epithet. Although a specific epithet may be repeated from one genus to the next, eg., *Magnolia virginiana* for Sweet Bay and *Fragaria virginiana* for the Wild Strawberry, the generic names are different and indicate that the plants are different—in this case they even belong to different plant families, the Magnolia family (Magnoliaceae) and the Rose family (Rosaceae) respectively.

In those cases in which a plant is given one scientific name by one botanist and another scientific name by another, the difference can be explained in one of two ways. Since 1930 considerable agreement has been reached, on an international level, concerning the rules for naming plants. Although aimed at ultimate stability, the new international rules have necessitated many changes in names that were used by botanists in this country before 1930. Those earlier names that have been replaced are now legally invalid. Another situation, involving botanical opinion rather than rules, often occurs if a species is quite variable or is poorly known. Under such conditions, different acceptable botanical interpretations of the presumed relationships result in two concepts and thus two names. Further taxonomic research might shed more light on the patterns of plant variation and relationship and ultimately resolve the problem. Even so, botanical names are far more uniform and stable, the world over, than common names and therefore they are given here, as are the scientific family names, to aid those who might wish to pursue the subject further.

The scientific name is followed by the name of the botanist who first described and classified the plant. This latter entry may be either a name or an abbreviation and may consist of one or two names, the first of which is then in parentheses. This indicates that a second botanist brought about some change in the status of the botanical name after it was first applied by the original author, whose name appears in the parentheses. These author, or authority, names are important to botanists as bibliographic references. For example, "Walter" after a plant name indicates that the plant was named by Thomas Walter, whose classic *Flora Caroliniana* was published in 1788. In a similar way "Linnaeus" or "L." after a plant name indicates that the plant was named by the Swedish botanist Carolus Linnaeus, who published many plant names and descriptions in his *Species Plantarum* in 1753. The large number of our plants first described by Linnaeus (1707-78), William Bartram (1739-1823) of Pennsylvania, Thomas Walter (1740-89) of South

Carolina, and the French botanist-explorer André Michaux (1746-1802) reflects the extensive early botanical exploration of eastern North America in general and of the Carolinas in particular.

Native vs. *introduced*

In most cases the botanical literature is complete enough to show which plants now growing in our area without cultivation are truly native and which have been introduced from other areas, chiefly Europe. This information is given, in either direct or indirect form, for each species. It is often coupled with information on the life span of the plant: whether it is *annual* and lives only one year or one season, *biennial* and lives for two years (usually blooming the second year, when it then sets seeds and dies), or *perennial* and lives for three or more years.

Scale or plant size

In each entry, reference is made to the size of the entire plant, or to some specific part, in order to give an idea of the scale of the picture and to aid in identification of the plant. The size ranges given are general and may, of course, vary somewhat depending upon environmental conditions. For more precise measurements and more complete descriptions, reference may be made to the *Manual of the Vascular Flora of the Carolinas* by index number as indicated below.

General comments

Here are included brief comments considered to be of particular interest or value concerning the specific plant illustrated, as well as comments regarding other closely related, and often similar, species found in North Carolina.

Frequency

Information on frequency (common, frequent, rare), though subjective and difficult to apply in many particular cases, is nonetheless included as a relative guide. This knowledge is of especial importance in respect to our rarer native plants that are in danger of becoming extinct. Such plants, now on the conservation list, are marked by an asterisk (*) beside the common name to encourage you to help with their preservation in their natural habitat.

Habitat

Usually our native wild flowers grow only in the particular habitats to which they are adapted. In order to help you know where to look for certain plants and to aid in the identification of others you may find unexpectedly, the habitat is given for each species treated.

Range in North Carolina

Varying environmental conditions in North Carolina's three geographic province—mountains, piedmont, and the coastal plain (Fig. 1.)—also influence plant distribution. As shown in Table 1, some species are limited to one or two of these provinces while others may be found throughout. For this reason knowledge of a plant's usual range may aid in the discovery and identification of the flowers treated here. If an entry reads "chiefly mountains," it means

Table 1. Distribution by province and relative frequency of the 2945 species of flowering plants of North Carolina

Number of Species Found In:	*Three or Fewer Counties*	*Four or More Counties*	*Total Species*
Mountains Only	171	142	313
Both Mountains and Piedmont	31	313	344
Piedmont Only	138	45	183
Both Piedmont and Coastal Plain	55	516	571
Coastal Plain Only	206	263	469
Both Coastal Plain and Mountains	8	26	34
Throughout	6	1025	1031
TOTALS	615	2330	2945

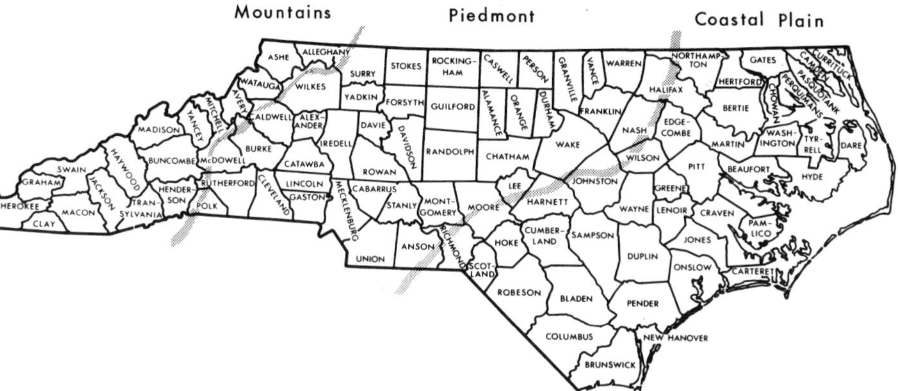

Figure 1. Map of North Carolina showing counties and provinces.

that most of the known localities for this species in our state are in the mountains but that a few are also known from the piedmont; "chiefly coastal plain and piedmont" would indicate primary distribution in these provinces but with a few localities in the mountains; "scattered throughout" means just that—specimens are found here and there in each of the three provinces.

General range

To illustrate the diversity of the regions of origin of our plants and to make this book more useful to those in areas adjacent to North Carolina, some indication is given of the general range of each species considered. Although an entry may say "more common northward" and thus indicate a north or northeastern center of primary distribution, the plant might also be found, though less frequently, southward in the mountains to northern Georgia or even northeastern Alabama. Likewise, a "southeastern species" may extend sporadically up the coast to Maryland or even southern New England.

Months in bloom

The last informational entry gives, in italics, the months in which the plant is normally in bloom in North Carolina. The entry *May-June* would indicate that the plant bloomed in our area during part or all of May and June. Of course, for plants of a species found throughout the state, those in the mountains will usually bloom later than those at lower elevations.

Index number

For those who might desire more specialized or detailed information on a plant or its relatives, the number at the end of each entry is provided as a handy index to each species in the *Manual of the Vascular Flora of the Carolinas.* For example the index number of Black Locust, 98-32-1, would refer to the *Manual* family number 98 (Fabaceae), genus 32 (*Robinia*) in this family, and species number 1 (*Robinia pseudo-acacia*) in this genus. The sequence of the plants illustrated in this book thus follows the botanical sequence, based on general relationships, that is found in the *Manual.*

The information on distribution in North Carolina is primarily from the *Atlas of the Vascular Flora of the Carolinas.* Blooming dates and habitats for each species are based on the *Guide to the Vascular Flora of the Carolinas* supplemented by field observations of the authors. The data on the general range of each species comes from the general botanical literature.

FLOWER STRUCTURE AND FUNCTION

Not all plants have flowers. The lower or more primitive types, algae, fungi, mosses, and ferns, do not produce flowers or seeds in their reproductive process. Pines and their relatives do form seeds but still have no structure that can be correctly called a flower. Only the more highly evolved plants—known botanically as the Angiosperms—have the specialized, complex, and often beautiful structures we call flowers.

A typical flower (Fig. 2.) is made up of four sets of parts, arranged in whorls or in concentric rings. Each part of the flower is specialized for a particular function. The outermost series of parts is the *calyx,* which is made up of the *sepals.* The calyx, in which the individual sepals may be entirely separate or fused to varying degrees, protects the flower in bud, and is usually green. The second whorl or series of parts is the *corolla,* which is made up of the *petals,* which also may be either fused, as in the Morning Glory and Rhododendron, or separate, as in the Lily and Cactus. The corolla is usually the most colorful part of the flower, the color, shape, and scent serving to attract the insects or birds often

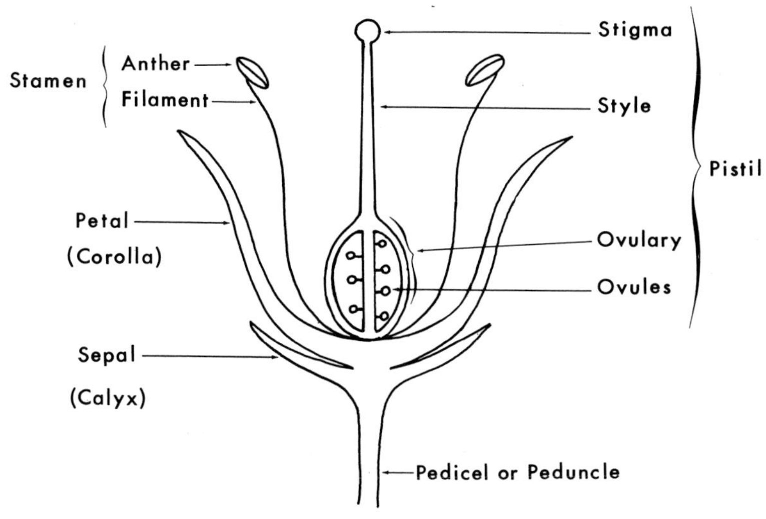

Figure 2. A diagrammatic section showing the parts of a typical flower.

necessary for *pollination,* which is the transfer of pollen from the anthers to the stigma. The third whorl is composed of the *stamens,* each of which bears a pollen sac, or *anther,* at the end of a slender *filament.* The pollen produces the cells that function as the male gametes. At the center of a typical flower is the *pistil,* or female reproductive portion, made up of three parts: the pollen receptive area, the *stigma*; a region of connective tissue, the *style*; and the ovule producing portion, the *ovary* or *ovulary.* The ovules, after fertilization, will develop into *seeds* and the ovulary will become the *fruit.*

Not all flowers, however, have all of these parts. Some, for example, have no petals. In these cases the flowers are frequently small, insignificant, and not very pretty. Such flowers would offer little attraction to pollinating insects. Thus it is not surprising to find that the pollen of these *apetalous* flowers is spread by the wind. Grasses, many trees (such as the oaks and willows), and even some plants in the Aster family (such as the familiar Ragweed) lack showy petals and are wind pollinated. On the other hand, some plants having flowers without petals or with insignificant ones are nontheless insect pollinated. When this is true, other structures have usually been modified through change in color and shape to function as "petals." Such is the case with Clematis, in which the sepals are colorful and petal-like, and in Dogwood, in which we find that the "flower" is actually made up of a cluster of small inconspicuous flowers surrounded by four showy white modified leaves or *bracts.* Another type of "flower" is found in such plants as Skunk Cabbage and Jack-in-the-Pulpit. In the case of these two, many small flowers are borne on a fleshy stalk, called the *spadix,* surrounded by a colorful envelope of tissue called the *spathe.* The color, shape, and odor of the spathe attract the pollinators.

A flower with both stamens and pistils, as in our illustration, is said to be *perfect.* However, the flowers of some plants are found to be unisexual; that is, they may be either *staminate,* with stamens only, or *pistillate,* with pistils only. If both male and female, or staminate and pistillate, flowers are found on a single plant it is said to be *monoecious.* If the male flowers are produced on one plant and the female flowers on another, as in the case of Holly, the plants are said to be *dioecious.* Most of the wind-pollinated plants mentioned earlier are either monoecious or dioecious and produce many more male than female flowers. The long clusters of male flowers, called catkins, are conspicuous on our alders, oaks, and hickories in early spring; the relatively few, small female flowers are rarely noticed.

Flowers are modified through adaptive changes in the shape, size, and relationship of parts as well as through the loss of parts. Flowers in the Lily family, Liliaceae (Fig. 3a), the Rose family, Rosaceae (Fig. 3b), and the Potato family, Solanaceae (Fig. 3c), are *actinomorphic.* That is, they are quite regular or radially symmetrical. In contrast, the flowers in the Orchid family, Orchidaceae (Fig. 4a), the Legume family, Fabaceae (Fig. 4b), and the Mint family, Lamiaceae (Fig. 4c), typically offer examples of *zygomorphic* flowers or flowers that have a bilateral symmetry.

Inflorescence is used as a general term to indicate the specific flower-bearing portion of the plant and usually refers to the particular type of arrangement of the flowers on the stems and branches (Fig. 6). The "flower" of the Jack-in-the-Pulpit, for example, is really a group of flowers in a specialized arrangement or inflorescence, and in the Aster family we also find that many "flowers," such as the common Daisy and the Black-eyed Susan, are not single flowers at all but are groups of flowers in a compact inflorescence or head. Furthermore, such heads often contain both actinomorphic and zygomorphic flowers. Each "petal" of a daisy is actually a separate flower (called a *ray* flower), with one large white petal. The center of the daisy is made up of many regular, small, yellow flowers (called *disc* flowers) with uniform petals (Fig. 5).

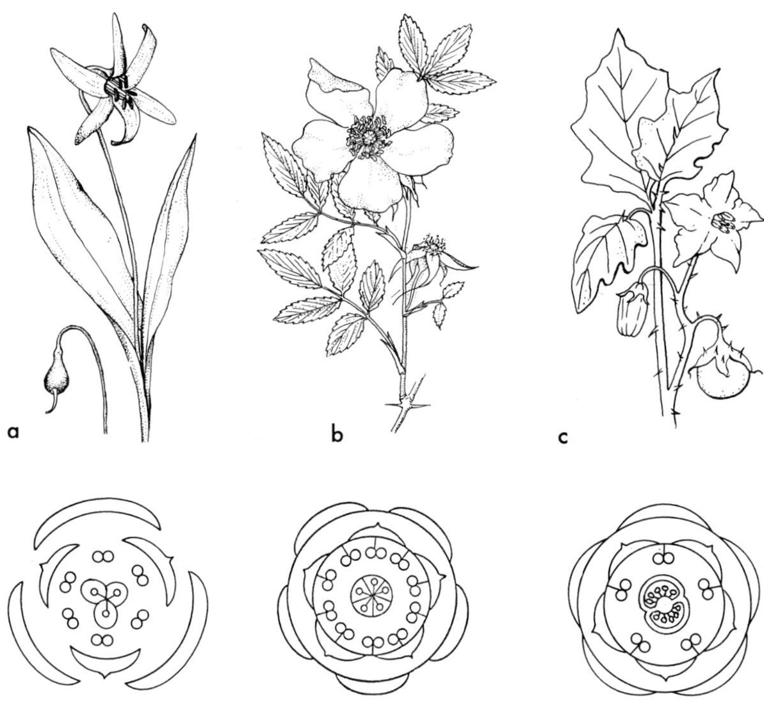

Figure 3. Examples of flowers with radial symmetry. The "floral diagrams" below each drawing represent schematically a cross section of the flower shown as representative for the family. The diagrams show the characteristic number and arrangement of the floral parts (sepals, petals, stamens, pistil) in each whorl of the flower. Such diagrams are often useful aids in plant identification. (a) Trout Lily *(Erythronium americanum)* Lily family (Liliaceae); a monocotyledon with parallel venation in the leaves and flower parts in sets of 3; the leafless flowering stalk of this plant is a good example of a scape. (b) Carolina Rose *(Rosa carolina)* Rose family (Rosaceae); a dicotyledon with net-veined leaves and flower parts in sets of 5, except for the fact that in this family there are usually many stamens; note the pinnately compound leaves with stipules at the base. (c) Horse Nettle *(Solanum carolinense)* Potato family (Solanaceae); a dicotyledon; the floral diagram indicates the sepals are fused, the petals are fused, and the stamens arise from the fused lower part of the corolla. (From *Plant Variation and Classification,* used by permission)

The flowering plants are divided into two major groups on the basis of minute internal differences, but members of each group usually can be recognized on the basis of flower structure, or flower structure in association with leaf structure. Monocotyledons (plants with only a single embryonic leaf, such as the lilies, orchids, and

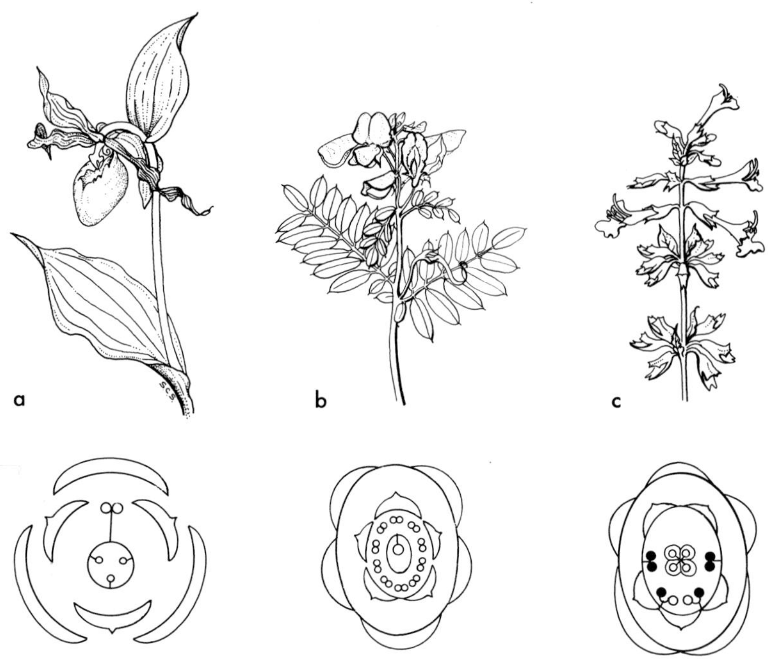

Figure 4. Examples of flowers with bilateral symmetry. The "floral diagrams" reflect the zygomorphic nature of the flowers, as well as the number and arrangement of the flower parts. (a) Yellow Lady Slipper (*Cypripedium calceolus*) Orchid family (Orchidaceae); another monocotyledon with typical parallel veins in the leaves and flower parts in sets of 3, but note in diagram the single stamen characteristic for the family fused to the pistil. (b) Goat's Rue (*Tephrosia virginiana*) Bean family (Fabaceae); a dicotyledon with reticulate veins in the leaflets of the pinnately compound leaves and with flower parts in sets of 5. (c) Lyre-leaved Sage *(Salvia lyrata)* Mint family (Lamiaceae); a dicotyledon; the sterile stamens of this plant are shown in black in the diagram. (From *Plant Variation and Classification,* used by permission)

grasses) generally have flower parts in 3's and the veins of the leaves are more or less parallel; dicotyledons (plants with two embryonic or seed leaves, such as the mustards, asters, and mints) generally have flower parts in 4's or 5's or in multiples of 4 or 5, and the veins of their leaves are reticulate or net-like and not parallel. In a similar way, with practice and careful application, different combinations of structural patterns enable us to distinguish individual plants and to assign them to their proper families. The variations in structure between unrelated plants and the similarities within groups are used by botanists in both identification and classification.

Plants of a given area can be identified by the use of a "key" or orderly list of contrasting characters by means of which the plant under consideration may be assigned to smaller and smaller groups until it is ultimately identified. However, a "key" for only four

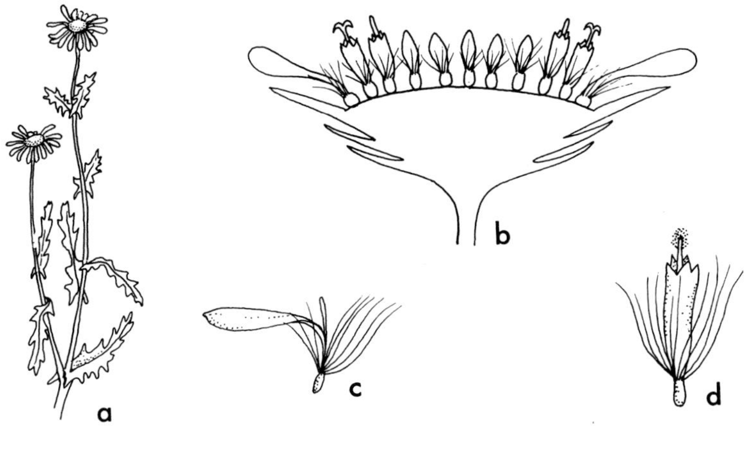

Figure 5. Flowers of the Aster family (Asteraceae). (a) Habit sketch of Ox-eye Daisy *(Chrysanthemum leucanthemum)*; (b) a diagrammatic section through a daisy head or inflorescence showing the two different kinds of flowers: ray flowers (c) are the zygomorphic outer flowers or "petals" of the dasiy, and disc flowers (d) are the radially symmetrical inner flowers that form the yellow center of the inflorescence. In (b) the disc flowers are shown in different stages of development; note the bracts shown on the receptacle just below the flowers. (From *Plant Variation and Classification,* used by permission)

hundred of our nearly three thousand flowering plants would be inaccurate and misleading. For that reason, in addition to the deliberate avoidance of a technical approach in this presentation, such a device has been omitted. Complete keys for the identification of all of our flowering plants can be found in the *Manual,* and, as pointed out in a previous paragraph, for your convenience each species illustrated in this little book is co-ordinated by reference number to the more detailed material in the *Manual.*

GLOSSARY

ACTINOMORPHIC. Regular, radially symmetrical; descriptive of a flower, or of a set of flower parts, that can be cut through the center into equal and similar parts along two or more planes.

ALTERNATE LEAF ARRANGEMENT. A single leaf per node.

ANGIOSPERM. One of the flowering plants (ovules enclosed in an ovulary).

ANNUAL. Life cycle completed in one year or less.

ANTHER. The fertile part of the stamen; the part that produces the pollen.

AXIL, LEAF. The angle formed between the stem and the upper surface of the leaf.

AXILLARY. In an axil.

BERRY. A simple, fleshy fruit in which the ovulary wall remains succulent.

BIENNIAL. A plant that completes its life cycle in two years and then dies; normally remains as a vegetative rosette the first year, flowering the second year.

BILABIATE. Two-lipped, as some corollas that are thus zygomorphic.

BLADE. The expanded or flattened part of the leaf.

BRACT. A reduced leaf, particularly one subtending a flower, or inflorescence, as the involucral bracts in the Aster family.

BUD. An aggregation of undeveloped leaves, or flowers, or both, on an axis with undeveloped internodes, often enclosed by scales.

CAMPANULATE. Bell-shaped, as some corollas.

CAPSULE. A dry, dehiscent fruit derived from two or more united carpels.

CATKIN. A scaly bracted, usually flexuous spike or spike-like inflorescence, often of unisexual flowers.

CLEFT. Cut ¼ to ½ the distance from the margin to midrib, or apex to base, or generally, any deep lobe or cut.

CORM. A bulb-like underground structure in which the fleshy portion is predominantly stem tissue and is covered by membranous scales.

COROLLA. The part of the flower made up of petals.

CORYMB. Short, broad, more or less flat-topped, indeterminate inflorescence, the outer flowers opening first.

DETERMINATE. Of limited or definite growth or size; an inflorescence in which the terminal flower matures first.

DICOTYLEDONS. Plants in one of the two subgroups of the angiosperms; characterized by two cotyledons in the embryo.

DIOECIOUS. Having the male and female reproductive organs on separate plants.

DIVIDED. Cut ¾ or more the distance from the leaf margin to midrib, or petal apex to base, or generally, any deep cut.

ENDEMIC. Restricted to a relatively small area or region.

ENTIRE. A margin without teeth, lobes, or divisions.

EPHEMERAL. Lasting only a short time.

EPIPHYTIC. A plant growing upon another plant, but not as a parasite.

FERTILE. A flower, or flower part, bearing functional reproductive structures.

FLORA. A collective term to refer to all of the plants of an area; a book dealing with the plants of an area.

FLOWER. An aggregation of highly modified fertile and sterile leaves making up the characteristic reproductive structure of angiosperms.

FLOWER, COMPLETE. A flower in which all four parts (calyx, corolla, stamens, and pistil) are present.

FLOWER, INCOMPLETE. Flowers in which one or more whorl or group of parts is missing.

FLOWER, PERFECT. A flower that contains both male and female reproductive organs; it need not have sepals and/or petals and may thus be incomplete.

FOLLICLE. A dry fruit, from a single ovulary, that splits open along a single line.

FRUIT. A matured ovulary with or without accessory structures.

GLABROUS. Without trichomes or hairs.

HERB. A plant with no persistent woody stem above ground.

HERBACEOUS. Plant parts with little or no hard, woody (secondary) tissue.

HERBARIUM. A collection of pressed, dried plants, and supporting information, filed by family, genus, and species for use in research and teaching.

INDETERMINATE. Not of limited growth or size; not determinate.

INVOLUCRE. A whorl or collection of bracts surrounding or subtending a flower cluster or a single flower.

LABIATE. With lips, as the bilabiate corolla of many mints.

LANCEOLATE. Lance-shaped, much longer than wide, widened at or above the base and tapering to the apex.

LEAF. The flattened, usually green, vegetative organ consisting of a distal blade (the flattened part) and a stalk or petiole.

LEAF, COMPOUND. A leaf in which the blade is subdivided into two or more leaflets; compound leaves may be pinnate, bipinnate, or palmate.

LEAF, SIMPLE. A leaf with only one blade, not compound.

LEAFLET. A single unit or division of a compound leaf which will ultimately separate from the leaf axis by an abscission layer.

LEGUME. A simple, dry, dehiscent fruit splitting along two sutures; characteristic of the Fabaceae or Bean family.

LOBED. Cut from ⅛ to ¼ the distance from the margin to midrib, or apex to base, or more generally, any cut resulting in rounded segments.

MONOCOTYLEDON. Plants in one of the two subgroups of the angiosperms; characterized by one cotyledon in the embryo.

MONOECIOUS. Having both kinds of incomplete (unisexual) flowers borne on a single plant.

NODE. The point on a stem at which one or more leaves are produced.

OPPOSITE LEAF ARRANGEMENT. Two leaves at a single node.

OVULARY. The fertile part of the pistil, enclosing the ovules, often called ovary.

OVULE. The structure occurring inside of the ovulary that contains the egg cell or female gamete; after fertilization it becomes the seed.

PAPPUS. The modified calyx lobes in Asteraceae.

PARALLEL VENATION. Leaf venation in which the major veins (vascular bundles) are parallel with one another; relatively characteristic of monocotyledons.

PARASITE. A plant that gets its food from another living organism.

PARTED. Cut from ½ to ¾ the distance from the margin to midrib or apex to base, or more generally, any moderately deep cut.

PEDICEL. The stalk of an individual flower in an inflorescence.

PEDUNCLE. The stalk of a flower cluster or of a single flower if the inflorescence consists of a single flower.

PELTATE. With the petiole joining the blade near the center rather than at the margin.

PERENNIAL. Plant of three or more years duration.

PERFOLIATE. A sessile leaf or bract whose base completely surrounds the stem, the latter seemingly passing through the leaf.

PERIANTH. The calyx and corolla of a flower.

PETAL. One of the leaf-like appendages making up the corolla.

PETIOLE. The stem-like part of the leaf.

PISTIL. The female reproductive parts of a flower; the stigma, style, and ovulary collectively.

PISTILLATE. A flower with one or more pistils but not stamens; a female flower, flower part, or plant.

PLICATE. Folded, as a paper fan.

POLLINATION. The actual transfer of pollen grains from the anther of the stamen to the stigma of the pistil.

PUBESCENCE. A general term for hairs or trichomes.

PUBESCENT. Covered with short, soft trichomes.

RACEME. A simple, elongated, indeterminate inflorescence with pedicelled or stalked flowers.

RHIZOME. An underground stem, usually horizontally oriented and sometimes specialized for food storage.

SAGITTATE. Like an arrowhead in form; triangular, with the basal lobes pointing downward or inward toward the petiole.

SAPROPHYTE. A plant that gets its food from dead organic material.

SCAPE. A leafless or naked flowering stem.

SCAPOSE. Producing a scape.

SEPALS. The outermost, sterile, leaf-like parts of a complete flower

SERRATE. With sharp teeth pointing forward.

SESSILE. Without petiole or pedicel.

SPUR. A tubular or sac-like projection from a petal or sepal; also, a very short branch with compact leaf arrangement.

STAMINATE. A flower with stamens but no pistil; a male flower or plant.

STIGMA. The pollen-receptive, terminal part of the pistil.

STIPULE. The basal, paired, leaf-like appendages of a petiole, sometimes fused.

STYLE. The elongated, sterile portion of the pistil between the stigma and the ovulary.

SUBTENDING. Below or beneath, as the bracts subtending an inflorescence.

SUTURE. A seam, or a line of opening.

TAXONOMY. A branch of botany that deals with the classification and identification of plants.

TENDRIL. A slender twining appendage or axis that enables plants to climb.

TERNATE. In three; three-parted or divided, as some leaves.

TRICHOME. A plant hair; trichomes may be simple, stellate, or glandular.

TUBER. A fleshy, enlarged portion of a rhizome or stolon with only vestigial scales; true tubers are found in the Solanaceae.

UMBEL. An inflorescence with pedicels or peduncles (rays), or both, each arising from a common point.

URCEOLATE. Urn-shaped, as the corollas of some Ericaceae.

WHORL. Three or more leaves or flowers at one node; in a circle.

WHORLED LEAF ARRANGEMENT. Three or more leaves attached to a stem at a single node.

WING. A thin membranous extension; the lateral petals in Fabaceae and Polygalaceae.

ZYGOMORPHIC. A bilaterally symmetrical flower which is divisible into equal halves in one plane only, usually along an anterior-posterior line; not actinomorphic or radially symmetrical.

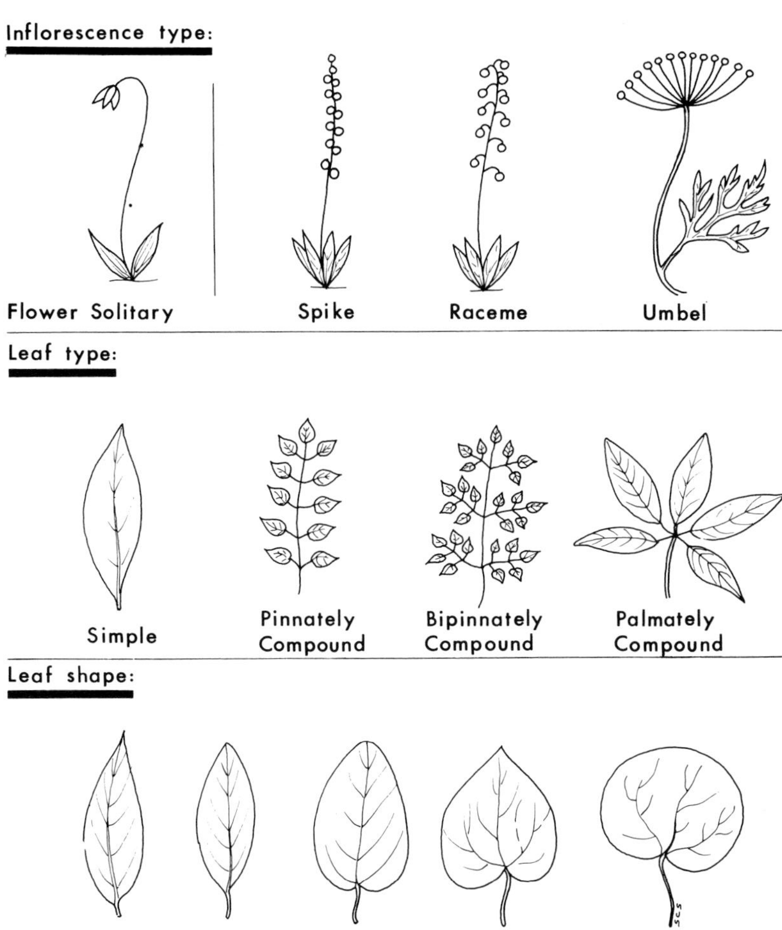
Inflorescence type:
Flower Solitary
Spike
Raceme
Umbel
Leaf type:
Simple
Pinnately Compound
Bipinnately Compound
Palmately Compound
Leaf shape:
Lanceolate
Elliptic
Ovate
Cordate
Reniform

Figure 6.

WILD FLOWERS

of

North Carolina

Typhaceae

CATTAIL

Typha angustifolia Linnaeus

The brown, compact, cylindrical "cattail," which is 6-8 inches long, is made up of hundreds of minute female flowers or, later, fruits. The many small male flowers form the spike above the female flowers but disappear soon after the pollen is shed.

Although this tall, rhizomatous, southeastern perennial is found in fresh or brackish marshes of our coastal plain, 3 other species of Cattail are found, collectively, throughout the state in the shallow water of rivers, lakes, and ponds. *May-July.* *(19-1-3)*

Alismataceae

DUCK POTATO

Sagittaria fasciculata E. O. Beal

Although the generic name implies that the leaves of plants in this genus are sagittate or arrow-shaped (see at bottom of next page) the narrow leaves of this species are lanceolate. In this respect it is somewhat similar to the following coastal species, but is smaller in all its parts; these flowers are about 1 inch across.

This native perennial is quite rare, occurring in swamps and upland bogs in only 2 of our mountain counties, where it may be endemic.
May-July. *(27-3-5)*

DUCK POTATO

Sagittaria falcata Pursh

Another *Sagittaria* with lanceolate rather than sagittate leaves. The leaves of these plants are 4-12 or more inches long. The underground stems contain a considerable quantity of starch and are eaten by animals.

These perennials are native to the tidal marshes, ditches, and stream margins of the outer coastal plain of North Carolina. Their general range follows the coast of the southeastern states.

June-October. (27-3-8)

ARROWHEAD; SWAMP POTATO

Sagittaria latifolia var. *pubescens* (Muhl.) J. G. Smith

Robust, native perennials 2-4 feet tall. The leaves in this particular species while often variable in size are always sagittate, which accounts both for the scientific name of the genus and for the first of the common names listed above.

Infrequent in bogs, wet ditches, and stream margins chiefly of the mountains and upper piedmont, but also at scattered localities on the coastal plain. Primarily a northern species.

June-September. (27-3-9)

SEA OATS*

Uniola paniculata Linnaeus

Drifting sand settles in the clumps of leaves of this native perennial grass that is frequently planted to help stabilize shifting dunes.

The graceful slender stalks, each 3-4 or more feet tall and bearing in summer and fall many flattened, yellow-brown or straw colored spikelets, are characteristic of the beach dunes and adjacent low open areas of the outer coastal plain. Virginia to Texas.

June-July. (29-10-4)

WILD RICE

Zizania aquatica Linnaeus

The long, slender, starchy grains produced by these plants are similar to the economically important grains produced by other plants of the Grass family and are considered a delicacy. The yellow to reddish brown anthers of the many male flowers are conspicuous when in bloom. The plants are 6-10 feet tall with sharp-edged leaves 1-3 inches wide.

Colonies of these native annuals are found in the brackish and fresh water marshes of our coastal plain and at scattered localities over much of the eastern U.S. *May.* (29-65-1)

SANDSPUR

Cenchrus tribuloides Linnaeus

Though few people have ever noticed the small flowers of this grass, many are painfully familiar with the spine-covered fruits. The burs of the plant shown are about ¼ inch across; the burs of our other 3 species are usually somewhat smaller.

A relatively frequent plant of the dunes and sandy clearings of the outer coastal plain. North Carolina to New York and to Louisiana.

August-October. (29-68-2)

BARNYARD GRASS

Echinochloa crusgalli (L.) Beauvois

Each of the compact, reddish brown racemes of Barnyard Grass is 1¼ inches or more long and help to identify this widespread species.

Plants of this introduced weedy grass are commonly found along open roadsides and in fields and waste places throughout North Carolina and much of the U.S.

July-October. (29-72-2)

Poaceae

PLUME GRASS; BEARD GRASS

Erianthus giganteus (Walt.) Muhlenberg

A coarse perennial usually 5-8 feet tall, with many small brownish red flowers in a colorful plume-like panicle that can be 18 or more inches long and 6 or more inches broad. Four other species of Plume Grass are also native to North Carolina.

The Giant Plume Grass illustrated grows on the savannahs, in moist ditches, and along woodland margins of the coastal plain and piedmont. Its general distribution is in the South Atlantic and Gulf Coast area.

October. *(29-85-5)*

Cyperaceae

SEDGE

Cyperus rivularis Kunth

Though grass-like, the sedges usually have solid, triangular stems rather than hollow, round stems as do the grasses. Flowers of both grasses and sedges are small and seldom noticed. In this sedge each compressed, reddish brown spikelet, only ¼-½ inch long, is made up of 12-30 small flowers or fruits.

This low native annual, a foot or less tall, forms symmetrical clumps in wet, sandy soil or gravel or in the peaty mud of low fields and ditches at scattered localities throughout the state and most of the eastern U.S.

July-September. *(30-1-5)*

WHITE BRACTED SEDGE

Dichromena latifolia Baldwin

Although the small flowers of sedges are relatively inconspicuous, the bright white bracts just below the inflorescence of this perennial, grass-like plant furnish a colorful contrast to the green of its other leaves and the surrounding low vegetation. The plants are 1-2 feet tall.

This is the rarer of our 2 species of *Dichromena,* both of which are native to the savannahs and wet ditches of our coastal plain. Both species are somewhat more abundant further south. *May-September.* (30-4-1)

Cyperaceae

COTTON-GRASS

Eriophorum virginicum Linnaeus

Despite the common name, this is a Sedge and not a member of the Grass family. When in fruit these plants produce many long, soft cotton-like bristles in a compact tawny mass, 1-2 inches across, which give them their common name.

A rare plant of our mountain or coastal plain bogs that is more frequent northward. *July-September.* (30-9-1)

Araceae

GOLDEN CLUB

Orontium aquaticum Linnaeus

Unlike the spadix of most other members of the Arum family, the long, white slender spadix of Golden Club is not enclosed by a spathe. The fertile portion of the spadix is the terminal 2-4 inches, which is golden yellow and bears many small, greenish yellow flowers.

Though chiefly found in bogs and along the margins of slow, acid streams of the coastal plain, these native rhizomatous perennials are also found at scattered localities in the piedmont and mountains. A plant primarily of the southeastern states. *March-April.* (32-2-1)

SKUNK CABBAGE

Symplocarpus foetidus (L.) Nuttall

The conspicuous aspects of this unusual looking "flower" are the large, somewhat fleshy, reddish brown spathe, which can be 6-8 inches long, and, as the name implies, a strong skunk-like odor. The color and odor attract flies and other pollinators to these plants. The large leaves, eventually 1-2 feet tall, appear with, or shortly after, the spathes and at first are rolled into compact cones.

Infrequent in bogs of our mountains and northern piedmont; native to northeastern North America. *February-March.* (32-3-1)

Araceae

ARROWLEAF; TUCKAHOE *(left)*

Peltandra virginica (L.) Kunth

The large glossy leaves of this robust native perennial may vary from 2 to 8 inches in width. The green spathe and later the greenish black fruits are characteristic of this common eastern species. Bogs, marshes, and wet ditches at scattered localities throughout the state. *May-June.* (32-4-1)

WHITE ARROW ARUM *(right)*

Peltandra sagittaefolia (Michx.) Morong

The bright white spathe and later the red fruits of this native perennial make it very showy. It is quite rare in North Carolina, which is the northern limit of this more southern species. Found in open bogs in only 3 coastal plain counties. *June-August.* (32-4-2)

GREEN DRAGON

Arisaema draconitum (L.) Schott

The large solitary, divided leaf of this native perennial usually has 7-15 segments and stands well above the rather inconspicuous "flower." The slender, tapered, greenish white spadix is 4 inches or more long and exceeds the spathe.

In low woods at scattered localities throughout the state and the eastern U.S. *May-July.* (32-5-1)

Araceae

JACK-IN-THE-PULPIT

Arisaema triphyllum (L.) Schott

The colorful green spathe, 2-4 inches long and variously striped with maroon, forms the "pulpit" that more or less encloses the erect, cylindrical spadix with its minute flowers. The spathe withers eventually exposing the fleshy, scarlet berries. The raw corm is very pungent but is edible when boiled.

These native perennials are found in low woods and bogs at scattered localities throughout the state and in much of the eastern U.S. *March-April.* (32-5-2)

Lemnaceae

DUCKWEED

Lemna perpusilla Torrey

WATER-MEAL

Wolffia columbiana Karsten

The small, flat plants of Duckweed and the still smaller plants of Water Meal, both shown here at about natural size, are among the smallest flowering plants in the world. Each flower is reduced to only a single stamen or a single pistil; there are no sepals or petals.

Duckweed is found floating on the surface of ponds, marshes, swamps, rivers, and lakes on our coastal plain. Water Meal may occur in the same habitats but is quite rare. Both plants are more frequent southward and rarely flower in our area. *(33-2-2) & (33-3-1)*

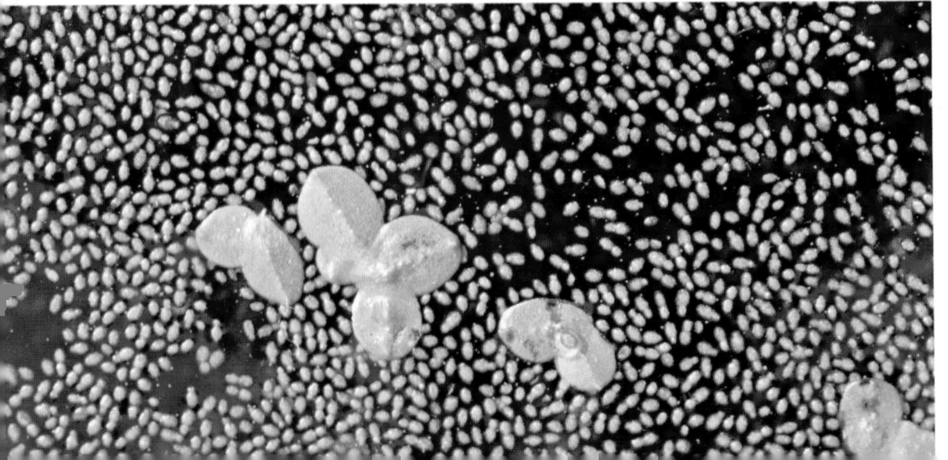

Xyridaceae

YELLOW-EYED GRASS

Xyris torta J. E. Smith

A slender, native perennial with grass-like leaves but with distinctive yellow flowers produced from compact, brown heads an inch or less long at the top of tall, leafless stems. Only 1 or 2 of the delicate flowers, often lasting for only a few hours, open on a spike each day.

Although plants of this particular species are found only in bogs, marshes, and wet ditches in the mountains, there are a dozen other species in similar habitats on the coastal plain. All are chiefly southern in general distribution.

June-August. (35-1-4)

Eriocaulaceae

PIPEWORT; HATPINS

Eriocaulon compressum Lamarck

The compact heads, made up of many small flowers, are about ⅓ inch across and are borne at the top of a slender stem 1-2 feet tall. The linear, parallel-veined leaves of these native perennials, arranged in a rosette at the base of the flower stalk, are generally similar in all 4 of our species of *Eriocaulon*. The dried heads remain white and are used in dried flower arrangements.

Infrequent at scattered localities, chiefly of the coastal plain. A plant primarily of the southeastern states.

June-October. (36-1-3)

DAYFLOWER

Commelina communis Linnaeus

The lower petal of these delicate flowers is white and greatly reduced, thus the corolla appears to be made up of only 2 petals. A flower lasts only a day or less, but other buds, within each green spathe (which is about ½ inch long and seen here just below the flower) continue to open for a week or more.

A weed of low, moist, often disturbed areas or waste places at scattered localities in the state and much of the eastern U.S. *May-frost.* (38-1-3)

PINK SPIDERWORT

Tradescantia rosea var. *graminea* (Small) Anderson & Woodson

The individual flowers of the Spiderworts, like those of the Dayflowers, last only a few hours. The two differ, among other things, in that Spiderworts have no spathe. The narrow leaves of this plant are less than ⅛ inch wide; the flowers are ¾ inch across.

Plants of this native perennial, which grows from Virginia to Florida, form grass-like clumps in the sandy, open woodlands of the coastal plain of North Carolina.

May-July. (38-3-1)

Commelinaceae

SPIDERWORT

Tradescantia subaspera Ker

A handsome, rather robust, fleshy native perennial 1-2 feet tall that often forms large clumps when growing under ideal soil and light conditions. The flowers, in which all 3 petals develop equally, are up to 1¼ inches across and vary from dark to light blue or even pinkish blue.

Infrequent in deciduous woods and clearings and along forest margins, chiefly in the mountains and piedmont. The general range of this species is the midwest. *June-July.* (38-3-2)

Pontederiaceae

PICKEREL WEED

Pontederia cordata Linnaeus

This somewhat rank native perennial produces a 3-6 inch spike of odorous, ephemeral flowers and glossy, usually wide leaves.

Relatively frequent in the shallow water of lakes, ponds, streams, and ditches, primarily of the piedmont and coastal plain. Found all along the east coast of the U.S. *May-September.* (39-2-1)

CARRION FLOWER

Smilax herbacea Linnaeus

The 1-2 inch round clusters of small green flowers are easily overlooked but the strong carrion odor, rather unexpected in a member of the lily family, cannot be missed. The flowers of this vine are pollinated by flies.

These native perennials are infrequent in swamp forests and wooded coves of our mountains and piedmont, and the northeastern U.S. The attractive fruit clusters are found in fall. *May-June.* (41-2-2)

GREENBRIAR; CATBRIAR

Smilax laurifolia Linnaeus

The thick, glossy, laurel-like, evergreen leaves of this native perennial vine are usually about 2-4 inches long. The tough, woody vines are spiny and often form dense thickets, or they may grow over and cover other vegetation.

Chiefly a coastal plain plant of southeastern distribution frequently found in bogs, moist lowlands, and low sandy-fill areas behind beach dunes. Various other species of *Smilax* also occur in North Carolina.
August-September. (41-2-10)

TRILLIUM*

Trillium cuneatum Rafinesque

The single flower of this plant has no stalk and is thus referred to as a sessile flower. One group of our Trilliums has such sessile flowers and the other group has flowers on short stalks or pedicels. The erect petals are about 2 inches long; the leaves up to 4 inches wide.

These native perennials, distributed throughout the southeastern states, are infrequent in the deciduous woods of the mountains and piedmont.
March-April. (41-3-1)

YELLOW TRILLIUM*

Trillium viride var. *luteum* Beck

These plants are similar to the foregoing species in all respects except color. Although some plants of this species in areas outside North Carolina have green petals, all of our plants are of the yellow variety.

A rare native perennial found in deciduous woods on limestone or basic soils in only 3 mountain counties. Because of the basic soil required by this plant its general range is roughly midwestern. *April-May.* (41-3-2)

Liliaceae

TRILLIUM*

Trillium discolor Wray

Another sessile Trillium that differs from the 2 preceding in color and petal shape. The various species of *Trillium* show more variation in the southern Appalachian region than elsewhere in their eastern North American range. A rare native perennial known from deciduous woods in one of our mountain counties and 3 piedmont counties in S.C. *April.* (41-3-3)

NODDING TRILLIUM*

Trillium cernuum Linnaeus

The flower stalk, or pedicel, of the Nodding Trillium is bent downward, thus the solitary flower is often hidden under the wide, spreading leaves. The leaves, which may each be 3-5 inches wide, later fold slightly upward and the 3-sided fruit is more exposed.

These native, herbaceous perennials, 8-24 inches tall, are found in deciduous woods at scattered localities in the mountains and piedmont. Their general range is northeastern. *April-May.* (41-3-5)

Liliaceae

CATESBY'S TRILLIUM*

Trillium catesbaei Elliott

The flowers of this pedicellate *Trillium* are about 1½ inches across and may be nodding or on a level with the short-petiolate leaves. Like all other species of *Trillium* it is a native perennial and is usually found in the deciduous woods and forests of the lower mountains and piedmont of North Carolina. A species of the southeast. *April-May.* *(41-3-6)*

WAKE ROBIN*

Trillium erectum Linnaeus

Although known as Purple Trillium, there is a yellow and a white form of this pedicellate species. The petals are 1-2 inches long. The flowers of the dark-colored form are ill-scented, and flies are attracted as pollinators by their maroon color and carrion odor.

These native perennials, chiefly northeastern in general distribution, are found in rich, moist woods of our mountains. *April-May.* *(41-3-7)*

WAKE ROBIN*

Trillium vaseyi Harbison

This plant is sometimes considered only a variety of *Trillium erectum,* which it resembles, except for the wider petals and longer filaments in its habitually nodding flowers.

These native perennials are infrequent in moist woods of their limited range in the mountains of the southern portion of the Blue Ridge in North Carolina, South Carolina, Georgia, and Tennessee. *April-June.* (41-3-7)

PAINTED TRILLIUM*

Trillium undulatum Willdenow

The white flowers, with the distinctive red inverted "V" at the base of each petal, make plants of this species easy to identify.

Although more common northward, these plants occur in bogs and hemlock or spruce-fir forests in our mountain counties.

April-May. (41-3-10)

Liliaceae

LARGE-FLOWERED TRILLIUM*

Trillium grandiflorum (Michx.) Salisbury

The flower of this striking and variable native perennial is on a short stalk or pedicel. The firm, white petals may be up to 2 inches long and turn pink as they age. The plants are 12-24 inches tall.

This Trillium is restricted to rich woods, usually on basic soils, in the mountains where it may be found at widely scattered localities, often in spectacular colonies. A species of the eastern U.S. *April-May.* *(41-3-8)*

INDIAN CUCUMBER-ROOT

Medeola virginiana Linnaeus

The two whorls of leaves and the nodding flowers about ¾ inch across, help identify this native perennial in bloom; the colorful change in the upper leaves and the dark blue berries with red pedicels identify it in the fall.

Occasional in moist, deciduous woods throughout the state and eastern U.S., but more frequent in the mountains. *April-June.* *(41-4-1)*

CLINTON'S LILY

Clintonia borealis (Ait.) Rafinesque

The leathery leaves of *Clintonia* are usually about 3 inches wide and have a strongly depressed midvein. The 4-8 cream or yellow flowers of this native perennial are ½-¾ inch long and form a loose cluster near the top of the slender scape or flower stalk; the berries are clear blue.

A more northern species found in North Carolina only in spruce-fir forests and on the heath balds at high elevations in the mountains.

May-June. *(41-5-1)*

SPECKLED WOOD LILY

Clintonia umbellulata (Michx.) Morong

This species, here shown in fruit, is very similar to the previous one but differs by having smaller, white petaled flowers only ¼-½ inch long, a more compact flower cluster, and ciliate or hairy leaf margins. The fruits may be dark blue to black.

A native perennial, more common northward, found at scattered localities in the wooded coves of our mountain counties. *May-June.* *(41-5-2)*

FALSE SOLOMON'S SEAL

Smilacina racemosa (L.) Desfontaines

The leaves of this native perennial are 2-3 or more inches wide and the flower cluster or inflorescence 4 or more inches long. The stem is conspicuously angled in a zigzag fashion from one set of leaves to the next. These plants are scattered in deciduous woodlands of eastern North America and are found throughout the state except on the outer coastal plain. *April-June.* *(41-6-1)*

FALSE LILY-OF-THE-VALLEY

Maianthemum canadense Desfontaines

The fragrant flowers of this low plant are quite different in shape from those of the true Lily-of-the-Valley, but the 1 or 2 dark green leaves, 1-3 inches wide, do somewhat resemble those of *Convallaria.* An infrequent native perennial, more widely distributed to the north, found in spruce-fir forests and wooded coves of the mountains. *May-June.* *(41-7-1)*

Liliaceae

NODDING MANDARIN

Disporum maculatum (Buckl.) Britton

These rare perennials may be 2 feet or more tall and the upper portion of the plant usually has numerous branches. The creamy white petals are nearly an inch long and, in this species, are spotted with purple.

Two species of *Disporum* occur in North Carolina. Both are more frequent northward and are found in our area only in wooded coves in the mountains. *April-May.* *(41-8-2)*

TWISTED-STALK

Streptopus roseus Michaux

These plants grow 1-2 feet tall and produce 1 or 2 small, rose flowers, ¼-½ inch long, from each axil of the upper leaves. The slender flower stalks of these native perennials have an offset, or bend, near the middle which accounts for the common name.

A more northern plant, infrequently found in spruce-fir forests and wooded coves of the mountains. *April-June.* *(41-9-1)*

Liliaceae

SOLOMON'S SEAL*

Polygonatum biflorum (Walt.) Elliott

The long, arching stems of this native perennial may reach 2-3 feet in length. It is easily distinguished from the False Solomon's Seal by the larger flowers, ½-¾ inch long, and later the black fruits, borne in small clusters along the stem rather than in a terminal inflorescence.

Plants of this widespread species of eastern North America are found scattered in deciduous woods and clearings generally throughout North Carolina. The fruits occur in early fall. *April-May.* *(41-10-2)*

Liliaceae

LILY-OF-THE-VALLEY

Convallaria montana Rafinesque

The 2 or 3 dark green leaves, 2-4 inches wide, and the small, white, bell-shaped and very fragrant flowers, characterize this species.

These low perennials, found in rich woods at scattered localities only in the Appalachian mountains, are somewhat different from the cultivated Lily-of-the-Valley and are presumed to be native. In North Carolina they are found, as indicated by the general range, only in the mountains.

April-June. *(41-11-1)*

SPANISH BAYONET; YUCCA

Yucca filamentosa Linnaeus

The leathery, linear, evergreen leaves of this species, usually 1-2 feet long and 1-3 inches wide, have slender filaments, or strands of fibers, along the margins. The flower stalk may be up to 6 feet tall.

A conspicuous perennial that is often cultivated. Native along the Atlantic coast from New Jersey to Florida, it is found in old fields and open woodlands at scattered localities in all provinces of North Carolina. Another species of Yucca is especially plentiful in the low sandy areas behind the beach dunes of our outer coastal plain.

May-June. *(41-12-3)*

TURKEY BEARD

Xerophyllum asphodelioides (L.) Nuttall

The grass-like clumps of basal leaves are easily overlooked and the spectacular flower stalks, which may grow to 4 feet tall, are sometimes chewed off by deer. Thus this rare plant is even more rarely seen.

In our area it grows in dry, open woods chiefly in the mountains. Its general range is primarily the Appalachian region and a portion of the coastal plain from New Jersey to Virginia. *May-June.* *(41-15-1)*

SWAMP PINK

Helonias bullata Linnaeus

The stout, hollow, flowering stem of the Swamp Pink is 1-2 feet tall and has many small, scale-like leaves or bracts. The larger evergreen leaves of this native perennial form a basal rosette.

A very rare plant of mountain swamps and bogs known from only 2 of our counties. The general range of the species is northward along the mountains. *April-May.* (41-16-1)

BLAZING STAR; DEVIL'S BIT

Chamaelirium luteum (L.) Gray

The plants of this species are dioecious, that is, one plant bears only female or pistillate flowers and another bears only male or staminate flowers. The staminate inflorescence of Blazing Star, with a drooping tip, is the more attractive and is shown here. It is often 4-8 inches long on a stalk 8-18 inches tall.

These native perennials are found in rich, deciduous woods at scattered localities throughout the state. They range generally over most of the eastern U.S. *April-June.* (41-17-1)

FALSE ASPHODEL

Tofieldia glutinosa Michaux

The slender flowering stalk, the upper portion of which is glandular and sticky, or glutinous, has a total length of 4-12 or more inches. The linear leaves are about ½-¾ as long as the stem.

Only 3 species of this native perennial occur in North Carolina. This more northern species is quite rare, found in bogs in only 3 of our mountain counties. The 2 other species, both found on the savannahs of the coastal plain, are southern in general distribution. *July-August.* (41-18-1)

PLEEA

Pleea tenuifolia Michaux

The slender flowering stems of this fall-blooming native perennial are 1-2 feet tall and about twice as long as the narrow, grass-like leaves. The delicate flowers are about ¾ inch across.

These plants are infrequent to rare in moist open, sandy areas of a few counties of the southeastern coastal plain of North Carolina where they may be found in association with Venus' Flytrap. The general range extends southward to Florida.
September-October. (41-19-1)

COLIC-ROOT

Aletris farinosa Linnaeus

The widely linear to lanceolate leaves, 2-6 inches long, form a basal rosette. The flower stalk grows from the center of the rosette and reaches a height of 18-30 inches. The small flowers have a granular or mealy appearance when observed closely.

Relatively frequent on the savannahs and moist, sandy roadsides of the coastal plain, more scattered in the moist woods and meadows of the piedmont and mountains, this species ranges more or less throughout the eastern U.S.

May-July. (41-20-2)

FLY-POISON

Amianthium muscaetoxicum (Walt.) Gray

The dense raceme is usually 2-4 inches long on a slender stalk 12-24 inches tall. The white petals and sepals do not wither after the flower has been pollinated but persist on the plant and turn green as they age. As the name implies, the plant is poisonous, especially the bulb.

A relatively widespread southeastern perennial found throughout North Carolina in bogs, savannahs, and deciduous woodlands.

May-July. (41-21-1)

POISON CAMAS

Zigadenus leimanthoides Gray

The open, branching inflorescence, 4-12 inches long, immediately separates this tall poisonous perennial from Fly Poison. However, there are 4 species of *Zigadenus* in North Carolina, and Crow Poison (Z. *densus*), which occurs on the coastal plain, does resemble the previous species.

A native of the southeastern states, these plants are quite rare in North Carolina and are known only from heath balds in 2 of our mountain counties.

July-August. (41-22-4)

BUNCH-FLOWER

Melanthium hybridum Walter

Another attractive but poisonous native perennial, the flowering stalk of these plants may be 3 feet or more tall; the linear basal leaves are much shorter and usually 2-3 inches wide.

Infrequent in deciduous forests at scattered localities in the mountains and piedmont of North Carolina. The general range of this plant is through the Atlantic Coast states south of New England.

July-August. (41-23-2)

FALSE HELLEBORE

Veratrum viride Aiton

A coarse, native perennial with a single leafy stem 2-6 feet tall bearing numerous yellow-green flowers. The wide, ovate leaves end in a sharp point and are strongly ribbed or plaited along the more or less parallel veins. All parts of this plant are poisonous, the roots being especially potent.

A northern species that is relatively frequent and conspicuous in bogs and moist woodlands of our mountain counties. *June-August.* *(41-24-1)*

FEATHER BELLS

Stenanthium gramineum (Ker) Morong

The single, tall, slender flowering stalk ends in a branched inflorescence of numerous, small, white to green flowers with linear sepals and petals about ¼ inch long. The flowers on the lateral branches are mostly staminate while those in the main or terminal spike are perfect.

Perennial herbs native to the southeast and found in moist meadows, bogs, and deciduous forests at scattered localities throughout the state.

June-September. *(41-25-1)*

Liliaceae

TROUT LILY; DOGTOOTH VIOLET

Erythronium americanum Ker

The wide, mottled leaves and the nodding yellow flowers with strongly recurved sepals and petals, immediately identify these native perennials that are among the earliest spring flowers.

A northeastern species often found in large colonies in open deciduous woodlands of our mountains and piedmont; it is rare on the coastal plain. *March-May.* (41-26-1)

ORANGE BELL LILY*

Lilium grayi S. Watson

The single stem of these plants is 18-36 inches tall and has several whorls of 2-3 inch long lanceolate leaves. There are 1-4 horizontal or slightly nodding flowers, each on a long stalk. The flowers, about 2½ inches long, are not strongly flared or reflexed.

A rare native perennial of the Alleghanies found in meadows and on balds in only a few of our mountain counties. *June-July.* (41-32-3)

CANADA LILY; MEADOW LILY*

Lilium canadense Linnaeus

The nodding yellow flowers with flared sepals and petals distinguish this species from the previous one. The leaf margins of plants of both of these species are finely serrate or scabrous.

A rare plant found as a native only in a few wet meadows and woodlands of some of our mountain counties. It is more common northward. *June-July.* *(41-32-4)*

TURK'S-CAP LILY*

Lilium superbum Linnaeus

Plants of this species may be 6 feet or more tall and bear a dozen or more nodding flowers. The strongly reflexed sepals and petals are green at the base and give the flower a dark center. The acutely pointed lanceolate leaves are usually widest near the middle and the margins are smooth.

A more northern native perennial found in moist meadows and wooded coves in our mountains. *June-August.* *(41-32-5)*

MICHAUX'S LILY; CAROLINA LILY*

Lilium michauxii Poiret

Although plants of this species appear similar to the Turk's-cap Lily they are smaller and have fewer flowers. Also, the petals lack the green basal markings of the Turk's-cap and the fleshy, obtusely pointed leaves are widest above the middle.

These native perennials, primarily southeastern in distribution, are found more or less throughout North Carolina in upland pine-oak woods and pocosins.

July-August. (41-32-6)

BELLWORT

Uvularia grandiflora Smith

The large, drooping flower, about 1½ inches long, is often almost hidden by the upper leaves, which are 2-4 inches long.

Scattered in forests of the eastern U.S. where calcareous or limestone soils are found. In North Carolina these perennials are found only in the mountains; 3 other species occur, variously distributed, throughout the state.

April-May. (41-33-2)

Liliaceae

NODDING ONION

Allium cernuum Roth ex Roemer

The scape, or flower stalk, is 8-24 inches tall, and the leaves of this native wild onion are flat and only about ¼ inch wide. This is much narrower than the 1 inch wide leaves of Ramps (*Allium tricoccum*) another native wild onion.

Relatively infrequent in deciduous woods and on granite outcrops of our mountains and piedmont. A species with a general range over much of the eastern U.S. where suitable habitats exist. *July-September.* (41-35-5)

Amaryllidaceae

SPIDER LILY

Hymenocallis occidentalis (LeConte) Kunth

These large flowers, 3-4 inches across, are made even more showy by the white "crown" of thin tissue that connects the bases of the anthers.

Two species of these native perennials occur in North Carolina. The species illustrated, with a generally central U.S. range, is extremely rare and is known from a moist habitat in only 1 upper piedmont county. The second, more southern, species, occurs in wet, often brackish habitats of the coastal plain. *June-August.* (44-2-2)

ATAMASCO LILY

Zephyranthes atamasco (L.) Herbert

These low perennials, 6-14 inches tall, have narrow, linear leaves and erect flowers about 3 inches long that rapidly change from pure white to pink as they age.

Though native to the southeast and usually found in wet meadows and low woods of the coastal plain and piedmont, these plants are present also in a few western counties, where their Indian name "Cullowhee" was given to one of our mountain towns.

March-May. (44-3-1)

YELLOW STAR-GRASS

Hypoxis hirsuta (L.) Coville

Low, grass-like, native perennials with pubescent leaves usually 4-10 inches long. The shorter flower stalk bears a loose cluster of 1-3 buds that open over a period of several days. The flowers are about natural size as shown here.

A widespread species of the eastern U.S., frequently found in open woodlands and meadows throughout North Carolina. The plants may be either solitary or scattered at a given locality. *March-June.* (44-6-1)

BLUE-EYED GRASS

Sisyrinchium angustifolium Miller

The 4-16 inch long flattened or winged flowering stems of these grass-like plants are much like the somewhat shorter leaves in appearance. These native perennials often form large clumps that produce many flower stalks. Despite the small size of an individual flower, here shown about twice natural size, the clumps are quite colorful.

A frequent plant in meadows and open, moist woodlands throughout the state and the eastern U.S. *March-June.* (46-2-4)

DWARF IRIS

Iris verna Linnaeus

The flowering stems of this species and the next are usually only 3-4 inches long, although our other *Iris* species have much longer stems. The orange band on the uncrested sepals and the relatively narrow, straight leaves distinguish this species from the Crested Iris.

This rhizomatous perennial is infrequently found in open, often rocky, woods at scattered localities throughout the state. A native of the Middle Atlantic region. *March-April.* (46-5-7)

Iridaceae

CRESTED DWARF IRIS

Iris cristata Aiton

Although the wide leaves of these plants may grow to a foot in length they are relatively short when the plants are in bloom. The sepals have a ciliate or pubescent crest in a white area near the base, and thus differ from the previous species.

An infrequent, rhizomatous, native perennial of rich woods of our mountains and piedmont. It occurs generally over much of the eastern U.S. *April-May.* *(46-5-8)*

Orchidaceae

PINK MOCCASIN FLOWER*

Cypripedium acaule Aiton

The inflated, lower petal forms a moccasin-like pouch 1½-2 inches long. The flowering stem of this species is leafless.

These native perennials often form large colonies in low pinelands and bogs chiefly of the mountains and coastal plain. Like other orchids, they will grow only when certain fungi, or molds, are present in their roots. If this fungus cannot survive in an area, the orchid will not live there either. A species of the mid-south area. *April-July.* *(49-1-1)*

Orchidaceae

YELLOW LADY SLIPPER*

Cypripedium calceolus var. *pubescens* (Willd.) Correll

These native perennials, 12-24 inches tall, may be either solitary or in spectacular colonies. The 3-5 alternate leaves on the flowering stem are 2-4 inches wide. The lip, or lower petal of the flower, is inflated to form a pouch 1-1½ inches long.

Infrequent or rare on rich wooded slopes of the mountains and a few scattered localities in the piedmont. Different varieties of this species occur throughout the eastern states. *April-June.* (49-1-2)

SHOWY LADY SLIPPER*

Cypripedium reginae Walter

The third, and rarest, of our 3 species of Lady Slipper, these coarse, pubescent plants are up to 2 feet tall and, like the previous species, have leafy flower stalks. The large ovate leaves are strongly ribbed; the flowers are fragrant.

A more northern species, native in swamps and on cool, wooded slopes in only 2 of our mountain counties. *May-June.* (49-1-3)

SHOWY ORCHIS*

Orchis spectabilis Linnaeus

The short scape, arising between the 2 wide, lustrous basal leaves, is usually only 3-4 inches tall but bears 3-10 showy flowers. The sepals and 2 petals are magenta, the third (lower) petal forms the flat, white lip.

A more northern species, rare along streams in rich hardwood (or rarely pine) forests of our piedmont and mountains.

April-May. (49-2-1)

GREEN FRINGED ORCHID*

Habenaria lacera (Michx.) Loddiges

The lacerated or finely cut lip of these small, fragrant flowers gives them the fringed appearance responsible for their name. The flower stalk is usually 8-24 inches tall with several oblong lower leaves 2-8 inches long and reduced, bract-like upper leaves.

An infrequent or rare native perennial in bogs, marshes, and wet meadows of the eastern U.S. In North Carolina it occurs chiefly in the mountains although known to be present at several stations in the other 2 provinces.

June-August. (49-3-1)

SMALL PURPLE FRINGED ORCHID*

Habenaria psycodes (L.) Sprengel

These native, somewhat variable perennials may be from 1-3 feet tall with elliptic leaves lower on the stem. The showy, compact raceme, 2-8 inches long, has numerous individual flowers each with a 3-lobed ciliate lip, about ½ inch wide.

Infrequent but easily seen in open woods, seepages and upland meadows of the North Carolina mountains. A species of chiefly northeastern distribution. *June-August.* (49-3-3)

PURPLE FRINGELESS ORCHID*

Habenaria peramoena Gray

The 3-parted lip or lower petal of these flowers is nearly 1 inch across. However, the margins of the 3 segments are only slightly serrate or toothed; they are not cut so deeply as to appear fringed, thus contrasting with the previous species. The raceme may be 6-8 inches long and 2-3 inches broad.

A rare orchid of the interior area of the southeastern U.S. which occurs in moist woods and meadows only in our mountains. *June-October.* (49-3-4)

WHITE FRINGED ORCHID*

Habenaria blephariglottis (Willd.) Hooker

The compact spike of this attractive orchid can be from 2-7 inches long on a stem usually 6-20 inches tall. The slender lip is finely fringed and contrasts with the entire, spreading sepals.

A rare to infrequent native perennial of bogs and moist, peaty depressions in savannahs and pine woodlands of the North Carolina coastal plain and 1 mountain county. A species of several varieties with a general range over much of the eastern U.S.
July-September. (49-3-13)

YELLOW FRINGED ORCHID*

Habenaria ciliaris (L.) R. Brown

A slender, native perennial 18-30 inches tall with linear to lanceolate lower leaves and a few reduced, alternate, stem leaves. The flowers, in spikes 2-6 inches long, each have a long spur and a deeply fringed, or ciliate, lip.

Infrequent and often solitary in bogs, meadows, and along the margins of thickets in the mountains and on the coastal plain. New England to the Carolinas and Georgia.

July-September. *(49-3-14)*

KIDNEY-LEAF TWAYBLADE*

Listera smallii Wiegand

The scientific name of this tiny orchid, only 4-10 inches tall, does not refer to its size but indicates that the plant was named for the botanist, J. K. Small, who discovered it. The 2 wide leaves are less than an inch long.

A rare plant of the Appalachian Mountains found in bogs, the humus of Rhododendron thickets, or on moist, wooded slopes in western North Carolina.

June-July. *(49-4-1)*

Orchidaceae

THREE BIRDS ORCHID*

Triphora trianthophora (Sw.) Rydberg

The 2-10 inch stem of this rather delicate native perennial usually bears 3 flowers, each about ¾ inch long, with spreading lateral sepals; from these characteristics the plant gets its common name.

Rare but apparently widely scattered in suitable habitats over much of eastern North America. These plants are found in rich, damp woods and thickets only in our mountain counties. *July-September.* *(49-5-1)*

LARGE WHORLED POGONIA*

Isotria verticillata (Willd.) Rafinesque

The very slender flower, with narrow, almost linear sepals, 1½-2½ inches long, arises directly from the center of a whorl of 5 wide leaves at the end of a stem 4-12 inches long.

A generally eastern U.S. species found in moist hardwood forests and along stream margins. It is infrequent at scattered localities throughout North Carolina. *April-July.* *(49-6-1)*

ROSE-CRESTED ORCHID*

Pogonia ophioglossoides (L.) Ker

The lip formed by the lower petal is a little less than an inch long and is densely bearded or crested. These native perennials, reported to 2 feet tall, are usually less than 1 foot tall. The single stem leaf is lanceolate, the basal leaves, absent at flowering, are lanceolate to oblong.

A plant generally ranging over much of the eastern U.S. at lower elevations. Found occasionally in North Carolina on savannahs, in bogs and low ditches, and on seepage slopes of the coastal plain and piedmont, rarely in the mountains. *May-June.* *(49-7-1)*

ROSEBUD ORCHID*

Cleistes divaricata (L.) Ames

The narrow, spreading, brown sepals of this perennial orchid are often 2-3 inches long and contrast sharply with the 2 fused, lavender, upper petals and the darker striped, slightly fringed lip. The stem is 12-18 inches tall with usually a single basal leaf and another single, firm or leathery, oblong leaf, about 4 inches long, halfway up the stem.

A southeastern native on the savannahs and damp pine barrens of the North Carolina coastal plain and in the upland woods of our mountains. *May-July.* *(49-8-1)*

BOG ROSE; BOG ARETHUSA*

Arethusa bulbosa Linnaeus

A low, native perennial growing from a bulb-like root. The solitary, terminal flower, 1-2 inches long, appears before the single linear leaf.

One of our rarest plants, it grows only in acid sphagnum bogs in the mountains. The southern limit for this species is North Carolina where, so far, it is known from only 2 counties though it is more frequent farther north. *May-June.* *(49-9-1)*

GRASS PINK*

Calopogon pulchellus (Salisb.) R. Brown

This plant gets its common name from its linear, grass-like leaves and 1-1¾ inch broad lavender-pink flowers. The slender flowering stem may be 1-2 or more feet tall.

Primarily a southeastern species but extending northward along the coast to New England or beyond, this perennial may occur in fairly large colonies in bogs, moist savannahs, meadows, and low grassy roadside ditches chiefly in our coastal plain and mountains. *April-July.* *(49-10-2)*

NODDING LADIES' TRESSES*

Spiranthes cernua (L.) L. C. Richard

The 2 rows of small flowers form a double spiral at the top of the flower stalk, which is usually 8-18 inches tall. The linear to lanceolate basal leaves may be 8 or more inches long.

These widespread and somewhat variable perennials are native to much of the eastern U.S. where they are found in varied moist, open habitats. In North Carolina they occur at scattered localities over the state.

July-frost. *(49-12-2)*

SLENDER LADIES' TRESSES*

Spiranthes gracilis (Bigel.) Beck

The single row of strongly spiralled flowers shows how this genus got its name. The slender spike is 1-4 inches long on a stem often 6-12 inches long. The leaves of these perennials are usually absent at flowering time. The lip of the small flowers is less than ¼ inch long.

Essentially a southern species found in dry to moist fields, meadows, and sandy hardwood forests of the mountains and piedmont of North Carolina.

April-September. *(49-12-4)*

RATTLE-SNAKE PLANTAIN*

Goodyera pubescens (Willd.) R. Brown

The compact spike of small flowers is 2-3 inches long, but another of our species has a spike only 1-2 inches long. Both have a basal cluster of dark green leaves marked with white along the veins.

A relatively abundant orchid found in small, isolated clumps or colonies in moist to dry coniferous or hardwood forests, chiefly of our mountains and piedmont. A species of the eastern U.S. *June-August.* (49-13-1)

LILY-LEAVED TWAYBLADE*

Liparis lilifolia (L.) L. C. Richard

A showy native perennial with 2 shiny basal leaves 2-5 inches long. Up to a dozen or more flowers may be in a single raceme.

Infrequent along stream-banks and on moist forest slopes; primarily found in our mountains and coastal plain. New England to the Carolinas. *May-July.* (49-15-1)

Orchidaceae

CRANE-FLY ORCHID*

Tipularia discolor (Pursh) Nuttall

The slender flower stalk, 8-16 inches tall, and the small brown and white flowers of this native perennial often escape notice. This is especially true since the characteristic ovate leaves, brownish green on top and maroon-purple beneath, are absent at flowering time.

Primarily a southeastern species, this orchid is rather frequent but inconspicuous in open deciduous woods throughout North Carolina.

July-September. (49-16-1)

Saururaceae

LIZARD'S TAIL

Saururus cernuus Linnaeus

The spike of small flowers, drooping at the tip, and the pointed, heart-shaped leaves are characteristic of these native marsh perennials that often form large colonies by rhizomes. The plants may be 1-3 feet tall.

A species of the eastern U.S. that often becomes weedy; found in stream and lake margins, swamps, and low woodlands of the coastal plain and piedmont.

May-July. (50-1-1)

Betulaceae

TAG ALDER

Alnus serrulata (Ait.) Willdenow

The reddish brown group of small, inconspicuous pistillate flowers of these wind-pollinated shrubs are above the narrowly cylindrical clusters, or catkins, of the staminate or male flowers that appear in this species early in spring before the leaves appear.

A common native of the eastern U.S., these plants are found along stream banks, marsh borders, and in other moist, usually open habitats throughout the state. *February-March.* *(54-1-2)*

Fagaceae

CHESTNUT

Castanea dentata (Marsh.) Borkhausen

Once the dominant tree of the eastern hardwood forests, this native has been wiped out by an introduced blight to which it was not immune. Today a few stump sprouts may grow large enough to bloom and set their spiny burs. Each bur is 1-3 inches in diameter and contains 1-3 sweet chestnuts.

These bushy stump sprouts can be found in our mountains and upper piedmont in dry, rich hardwood forests. *June.* *(55-2-1)*

Fagaceae

CHINQUAPIN

Castanea pumila (L.) Miller

These native shrubs or small trees, related to the Oaks, were fortunately not affected by the blight that wiped out their other larger relative, the Chestnut. The slender spike of strong-scented, staminate flowers is 3-6 inches long. The pistillate flowers are inconspicuous. The bur, about 1 inch in diameter, usually contains a single sweet nut.

Scattered in dry, deciduous woods of the southeast and throughout North Carolina but more frequent in the mountains. *June.* *(55-2-2)*

Santalaceae

BASTARD TOADFLAX

Comandra umbellata (L.) Nuttall

These low, herbaceous, perennials are partly parasitic on the roots of oak trees. The narrowly elliptic leaves are ½-1 inch wide and the small umbels of white flowers about ½ inch across.

A plant chiefly of the midwest, *Comandra* is found at scattered localities in the deciduous woodlands of the piedmont of North Carolina and also in a few counties of the mountains and coastal plain. *April-June.* *(60-1-1)*

Aristolochiaceae

BIRTHWORT; DUTCHMAN'S PIPE

Aristolochia macrophylla Lamarck

The small flowers of this perennial vine have no petals—the sepals form the strongly curved, pipe-like bloom that is over an inch long. The alternate, heart-shaped leaves may be up to 12 or more inches across though 4-8 inches is the more usual size. These interesting plants, primarily of the Appalachian region, are infrequent in the rich woods of our mountains. *May-June.* (62-1-1)

WILD GINGER

Asarum canadense Linnaeus

The thin, pubescent, heart-shaped leaves of this aromatic, native perennial are usually 2-4 inches wide but occasionally can be much larger. The flowers lack petals; the slender, pointed lobes of the maroon calyx are about ¼ inch long. Primarily a northeastern species found in our mountains in rich woods and at a few scattered localities in the piedmont. *April-May.* (62-2-1)

Aristolochiaceae

HEART LEAF; WILD GINGER

Hexastylis shuttleworthii (Britt. & Baker) Small

These perennial herbs also are aromatic but differ from *Asarum* in their fleshy flowers, wide-lobed calyx, and firm, glabrous, evergreen leaves.

One or another of our 8 species of *Hexastylis* occurs in the deciduous woods of nearly every county in North Carolina. However, the species illustrated, with flowers an inch or more across, is restricted to the Blue Ridge area and is found only in our mountains. *May-July.* (62-3-6)

Polygonaceae

SORREL

Rumex hastatulus Elliott

The small flowers of these dioecious annuals are crowded on the short branches of the inflorescence at the top of a stem that is usually 12-36 inches tall.

A common weed of old fields in the coastal plain, often in colorful association with the blue Toadflax. A native of sandy soils at lower elevations over much of the southeast. Several related weedy species have been introduced including the similar but smaller, more widespread, rhizomatous, perennial weed, Sheep Sorrel (*Rumex acetosella*). *March-May.* (63-2-2)

Polygonaceae

KNOTWEED; PINKWEED

Polygonum pensylvanicum Linnaeus

Although the compact, 1-2 inch long spikes of pink flowers are similar in most of the various species of *Polygonum* found in our area, some of the plants have small, wicked barbs on the slender stems and can inflict painful cuts. The common name for these plants is "Tearthumb." The stems of all our species of Knotweed are thickened at the nodes and appear jointed.

These variable weedy annuals, up to 3 feet tall, are found in usually moist fields, on roadsides, and in disturbed habitats throughout our state and much of the eastern U.S. *July-frost.* *(63-4-8)*

Phytolaccaceae

POKE

Phytolacca americana Linnaeus

These rank, herbaceous perennials may reach a height of 6 feet or more and have a spread to match. The plant may have racemes of small white flowers, green fruits, and the ripe fruits, as shown here, at the same time late in the season. The juice of the berries was once used for ink and the young, tender leaves are excellent when properly cooked. The root is poisonous.

These plants are frequent in low grounds and recent clearings throughout the state and the eastern U.S. *May-frost.* *(68-1-1)*

SPRING-BEAUTY

Claytonia caroliniana Michaux

These low, herbaceous perennials are usually 3-10 inches tall. Each corm may produce several to many flowering stems and each stem produces up to a dozen flowers with striped petals about ¼ inch long.

A native of the mountains of the eastern U.S., these plants are frequently found in the rich, deciduous woods of our western counties.

March-April. (70-1-2)

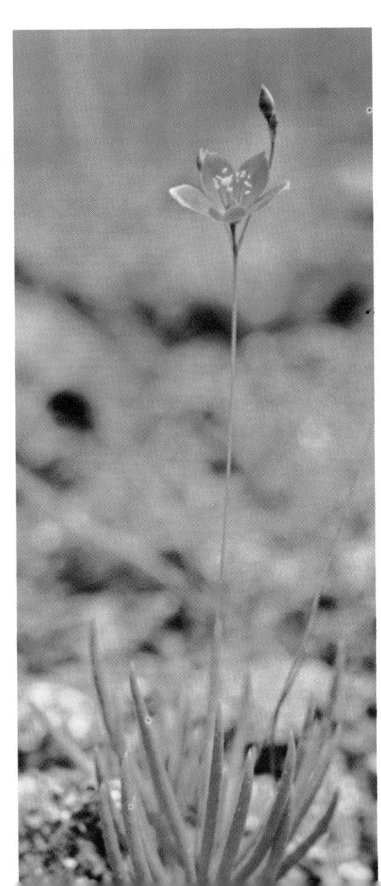

SEDUM

Talinum teretifolium Pursh

The fleshy, linear leaves are 1-2 inches long and are round, or terete, in cross section. The petals, each about ¼ inch long, drop soon after the flower opens.

These small perennials are native to the southeastern U.S. where they occur on rock outcrops and on dry sandy soils. In North Carolina they are found at scattered localities in the mountains and piedmont.

June-September. (70-2-1)

Caryophyllaceae

GIANT CHICKWEED

Stellaria pubera Michaux

The attractive flowers of this native Chickweed are about ½ inch across and appear to have 10 petals. On closer examination, however, it will be found that each flower has only 5 petals, as do other members of the Pink family, but each petal is parted or divided into 2 linear segments.

This southeastern perennial is relatively frequent in the deciduous woods of the mountains and piedmont of North Carolina. *April-June.* (71-7-4)

SOAPWORT; BOUNCING-BET

Saponaria officinalis Linnaeus

A robust, introduced perennial, 1-2 feet tall with flowers about 1 inch across. The first common name comes from the fact that the juice of the crushed stems forms a soap-like lather with water.

These plants are widely naturalized in this country. When well established they form large, rather showy clumps along roadsides, in old fields, and in waste places. They are relatively frequent at scattered localities throughout North Carolina. *May-frost.* (71-15-1)

FIRE PINK; INDIAN PINK

Silene virginica Linnaeus

The sticky stems of this native perennial have opposite leaves, are regularly branched, and are 1-2 feet tall. The showy flowers, with petals often deeply notched, are up to 2 inches across.

Single plants or clumps of Fire Pink are seen along roadsides at the edge of rich woods in the mountains and piedmont of North Carolina and over much of the eastern U.S. *April-July.* (71-17-7)

STARRY CAMPION

Silene stellata (L.) Aiton f.

The 5 petals of the ¾ inch broad flowers are less finely divided in this species and the upper leaves are whorled; in these respects it differs from the rarer species below.

These native perennials are infrequent, though they sometimes occur in large patches locally in, or at the margins of, rich woods in our mountains and piedmont. An eastern or northeastern species.

July-September. (71-17-1)

CAMPION

Silene ovata Pursh

The linear segments of the finely dissected petals of this native perennial are ¼-½ inch long. The plants, like those above, may be 1-3 feet tall; however, all leaves of this species are opposite.

A rare plant of the rich woods of the southern Appalachian area, known in North Carolina from only a few mountain counties.

August-September. (71-17-9)

Nymphaeaceae

COW LILY; SPATTER DOCK

Nuphar luteum (L.) Sibthorp & Smith

The leaves of these coarse, rhizomatous perennials are quite variable and may be wide or rather narrow. The flower is 1-2 inches across with a prominent, fleshy, lobed stigma. These natives of the eastern U.S. are found in ponds, rivers, and lakes at scattered localities, chiefly in our coastal plain and piedmont. *April-frost.* (73-1-1)

WATER-LILY

Nymphaea odorata Aiton

A sweet-scented, native, rhizomatous perennial with large leaves that are green above and usually reddish brown beneath. The flowers, which open for several days, are 3-6 inches across. A plant of the eastern U.S. found in North Carolina in lakes, ponds, and wet ditches at scattered localities, chiefly in the coastal plain.
June-September. (73-2-1)

WILD COLUMBINE*

Aquilegia canadensis Linnaeus

The nodding flowers, borne on slender stems up to 3 feet tall, are an inch or more long counting the deep spur at the base of each petal. The leaves are divided into 3 rounded segments that may be divided again into 3 segments.

A native perennial of the eastern U.S. that is found occasionally in rich, rocky woods at scattered localities throughout the state, but more frequently in the mountains.

March-May. (76-2-1)

LARKSPUR

Delphinium tricorne Michaux

In these flowers, which are about 1 inch long, the sepals instead of the petals are showy; the single spur is formed by the upper sepal. The fruit of this species is strongly 3-parted; the leaves are usually divided into 5 primary segments that may be further lobed or cleft.

This poisonous native perennial is infrequent, though often occuring in large colonies, in the rich woods of the mountains and lower piedmont of North Carolina. It is primarily a northeastern species.

March-May. (76-3-2)

Ranunculaceae

MONKSHOOD*

Aconitum uncinatum Linnaeus

Another poisonous member of the Buttercup family with a spurred upper sepal, the flowers of Monkshood are ½-¾ inch long. The leaves have 3-5 lobes that are less dissected than those of the *Delphinium*. These perennials, which are found in rich woods from Pennsylvania to northern Georgia, are infrequent in our mountains and northern piedmont.
August-September. (76-4-1)

MARSH MARIGOLD

Caltha palustris Linnaeus

No relation at all to the Marigold of our gardens (which belongs to the Aster family), these rare, showy, native perennials have golden, petal-like sepals nearly 1 inch long. A northern species known only from the marshes of a few of our mountain counties. *April-June.* (76-6-1)

BANEBERRY; NECKLACE WEED

Actaea pachypoda Elliott

These poisonous perennials are 1-3 feet tall, and each stem bears a compact cluster of small flowers. However, it is the fruit that is the more colorful (and more poisonous!) with the red pedicels and white berries. The compound leaves have ovate, sharply toothed leaflets.

These plants are primarily northern in distribution. They are native in the rich woods of the mountains and piedmont of North Carolina.

April-May. (76-8-1)

BLACK COHOSH

Cimicifuga racemosa Nuttall

The slender, graceful racemes of these native perennials may be 3 feet long and, since the flowers open in succession upward, a raceme may remain in bloom for 2 weeks or more. The total height of the flower stalk may be 4-8 feet, extending much above the large, compound basal leaves.

Relatively frequent in clearings in rich woods of the North Carolina mountains and piedmont, these plants are primarily northeastern in their distribution. *May-July.* (76-9-1)

Ranunculaceae

LEATHER FLOWER

Clematis viorna Linnaeus

The slender, silky fruits are more conspicuous than the nodding, 1 inch long flowers with their thick, fleshy, petal-like sepals. The compound leaves have 3-7 leaflets. A perennial vine chiefly of the central U.S. found along the margins of rich woodlands on basic or limestone soil in our mountains and piedmont.
May-September. (76-10-4)

VIRGIN'S BOWER

Clematis virginiana Linnaeus

A very showy, native perennial vine that is sometimes cultivated. The leaves have 3 leaflets, and the fragrant flowers, about 1 inch across, are rotate, or rather flat. A species of the eastern U.S. that is relatively infrequent along streams and in openings in low woods in our piedmont and mountains. *July-September.* (76-10-7)

Ranunculaceae

WINDFLOWER

Thalictrum thalictroides (L.) Boivin

The ¾ inch wide flowers of these low, delicate, early spring perennials may be either pure white or tinged with pink. A frequent inhabitant of rich, often low woods of most of the eastern U.S., these plants are found chiefly in our mountains and piedmont. *March-May.* (76-11-1)

MEADOW RUE

Thalictrum revolutum DeCandolle

Quite different in appearance from the small *Thalictrum* shown above, the flower stalk of these native perennials may be as much as 6 feet tall. The many small flowers, about ¼ inch long, are widely spaced and give the inflorescene a feathery appearance.

This species, primarily more northern in distribution, is found chiefly in the dry woods and meadows of the mountains and piedmont. Seven other tall, somewhat similar Meadow Rues occur in our state. *May-July.* (76-11-5)

Ranunculaceae

BUTTERCUP

Ranunculus hispidus Michaux

Several species of these handsome plants, some taller than this 6-18 inch perennial, occur in our area. The waxy, yellow flowers are about ½ inch across; the petioles and flower stems are hispid. This is a more northern species, found scattered in the low woods and meadows throughout our piedmont and mountains. *March-June.* (76-13-19)

HEPATICA; LIVERWORT*

Hepatica acutiloba DeCandolle

The new green leaves, appearing on these plants after the flowering period, persist through the summer and following winter, by which time they have turned bronze or reddish brown. The flowers are ½-¾ inch across and may be either pale blue, white, or rarely rose.

This northeastern perennial occurs rather frequently in the rich woods of western North Carolina. *March-April.* (76-15-1)

Ranunculaceae

HEPATICA; LIVERWORT*

Hepatica americana (DC.) Ker

Although similar in most respects to the previous species, the 3 leaf lobes of these plants are rounded instead of pointed. The flowers are usually lavender but may be white or rose.

These native perennials are relatively frequent in the rich woods of the piedmont but are less frequent in the mountains and coastal plain; they occur over much of the eastern U.S. *February-April.* (76-15-2)

THIMBLEWEED; WOOD-ANEMONE

Anemone quinquefolia Linnaeus

The flowers of these rhizomatous native perennials have firm white sepals about ½ inch long. The rounded cluster of small, densely woolly fruits is about ½ inch around. The stems and leaves are usually glabrous.

Primarily a northern species, these plants are found in rich woods and along woodland borders at scattered localities chiefly in the mountains. *March-May.* (76-16-3)

BLUE COHOSH

Caulophyllum thalictroides (L.) Michaux

These glabrous perennials, usually 18-30 inches tall have a single, large, much-divided leaf and a single flower stalk. The small greenish brown flowers are less conspicuous than the small, blue, exposed, poisonous seeds, which have grown faster than the ovary and have split it.

Though primarily more northern in distribution, these native plants are found in the rich deciduous forests of our mountain coves and at 2 localities in the piedmont near the center of the state. *April-May.* (77-5-1)

UMBRELLA-LEAF

Diphylleia cymosa Michaux

A single large, umbrella-like leaf, 1-2 feet across, is produced on non-flowering stems, and two somewhat smaller leaves appear on the flowering stems. The white flowers, each about 1 inch broad, are followed by round blue fruits a little more than ¼ inch in diameter. These rhizomatous perennials, which are found on rich seepage slopes only in the southern Appalachians, are infrequent in our mountain counties. *May-June.* (77-6-1)

Berberidaceae

MAYAPPLE; MANDRAKE*

Podophyllum peltatum Linnaeus

Flowering stems of these rhizomatous perennials have 2 roughly circular, 3-7 lobed, peltate leaves, 6-8 inches wide, with a single waxy flower, 1-2 inches across, between them. Flowerless stems have only a single leaf. The plants are medicinal but poisonous in too large an amount. Native to the eastern U.S., they are frequent in low, alluvial woods and moist meadows throughout North Carolina. *March-April.* (77-7-1)

Menispermaceae

CORAL BEADS

Cocculus carolinus (L.) DeCandolle

A slender perennial vine with small, greenish white flowers and alternate, weakly or strongly lobed leaves 2-4 inches long. The translucent, crimson berries, about ¼ inch in diameter, ripen in the early fall.

These vines, native to the southeastern U.S., are found in our area along fencerows and in fields and sandy woodlands of the coastal plain and piedmont. *June-August.* (79-1-1)

TULIP TREE

Liriodendron tulipifera Linnaeus

These large, handsome, and commercially important trees are immediately recognized by their brilliant orange and green, tulip-shaped flowers 1-2 inches broad and their wide leaves with a shallow notch at the end. A native of the eastern U.S., Tulip Poplars are found in coves or low, often recently cleared, woodlands essentially throughout the state. *April-June.* *(80-1-1)*

SWEET BAY

Magnolia virginiana Linnaeus

This is usually a medium to small tree or, in areas that have been frequently cut over or burned, a bushy stump sprout. The semi-evergreen leaves are 3-6 inches across, and the fragrant flowers 1-2 inches broad.

Primarily a native of the southeastern U.S., Sweet Bay is frequent to common on savannahs, in pocosins, and in roadside thickets chiefly of our coastal plain. *April-June.* *(80-2-1)*

Magnoliaceae

MAGNOLIA; BULL BAY

Magnolia grandiflora Linnaeus

This large evergreen tree has leaves 4-10 inches long that are glossy above and reddish brown and pubescent beneath. The fragrant flowers may be 12 inches across when fully open.

Although widely planted over a much larger area, this native of the southeastern U.S. reaches its natural northern limit in the swamp forests and low woods of southeastern North Carolina. *May-June.* (80-2-2)

UMBRELLA TREE; MOUNTAIN MAGNOLIA

Magnolia fraseri Walter

The leaves of this slender native tree are thin, deciduous, 6-18 inches long, and have a prominent notch at the base. The petals are usually 3-4 inches long. The leaves of the somewhat similar *Magnolia tripetala,* found scattered over the state, are not notched at the base.

A native of the southern Appalachians, these trees are found in rich woods of the mountains and upper piedmont of North Carolina. *April-May.* (80-2-4)

Annonaceae

PAWPAW

Asimina triloba (L.) Dunal

A low, slender, often bushy, native shrub. The thin leaves, odorus when bruised, are obovate, often 6-8 inches long, and appear after the maroon, 3-parted, 1-1½ inches broad flowers. The fleshy, fragrant fruit, 2-3 inches long, is edible.

A native of the eastern U.S., these trees are infrequently found in low woods at scattered localities throughout the state. *March-May.* *(81-1-2)*

Calycanthaceae

SWEET SHRUB; SWEET BETSY

Calycanthus floridus Linnaeus

This native shrub, often widely planted as an ornamental, has opposite, deciduous leaves that vary in color and texture. The flowers are an inch or more broad and have a spicy fragrance; the seeds are poisonous.

A plant of the southeastern U.S., this shrub is found on hills and stream banks at the margins of deciduous woodlands chiefly in our upper piedmont and mountains. *March-June.* *(83-1-1)*

Lauraceae

SASSAFRAS

Sassafras albidum (Nutt.) Nees von Esenbeck

The leaves, 3-6 inches long, may have 3 lobes, 2 lobes or none, all on the same tree. The aromatic root is used to flavor root-beer, and the finely powdered young leaves furnish the mucilaginous "gumbo" of Louisiana cooking.

A native of the eastern U.S. that is frequently found throughout our area as a low tree in cut-over areas along fencerows and woodlands. The clusters of yellow flowers appear before the leaves. *March-April.* *(84-2-1)*

Papaveraceae

BLOODROOT*

Sanguinaria canadensis Linnaeus

The poisonous rhizome of this low perennial has a bright, red-orange sap. The showy flowers have 8-12 petals 1-2 inches long. The usually solitary leaf, glaucous beneath, is 4-8 inches across and deeply cleft into numerous wide segments.

A native of the eastern U.S., Bloodroot is frequently found in open mixed deciduous forests chiefly of the mountains and piedmont.
March-April. *(85-1-1)*

POPPY

Papaver dubium Linnaeus

The showy petals of this introduced annual last hardly a day. The flower stalk seldom exceeds 1 foot in height; the smooth, club-shaped capsule is about 1 inch long.

Though rare in fields and on roadsides at a dozen scattered localities in our area, these plants appear to be thoroughly naturalized in the vicinity of Wilmington. *April-June.* (85-5-4)

Fumariaceae

BLEEDING HEART

Dicentra eximia (Ker) Torrey

A low perennial, about 16 inches tall, with drooping, flattened pink or rose flowers an inch or more long. The leaves are not as finely divided as in the following 2 species.

These plants, rare on rich, wooded slopes and in the coves and gorges of only a few of our mountain counties, have a general range centered around the Appalachians. *April-June.* *(86-2-1)*

SQUIRREL CORN

Dicentra canadensis (Goldie) Walpers

The roots of this low, native perennial form small, round, yellow tubers. Although the finely divided leaves of Squirrel Corn are similar to those of Dutchman's Breeches on the next page, the rounded, approximate basal spurs of the ¾ inch flowers serve to distinguish this species.

Primarily a northeastern plant, it is found infrequently on moist slopes and in wooded coves of the mountains, occasionally in large stands. *April-May.* (86-2-2)

Fumariaceae

DUTCHMAN'S BREECHES*

Dicentra cucullaria (L.) Bernhardi

Although vegetatively similar to Squirrel Corn, the basal spurs of the flowers of this species are ½ or more the total flower length and are also more divirgent. A native perennial, primarily of the northeastern U.S., found occasionally in rich woods and on north slope river banks in our mountains and piedmont. *March-April.* (86-2-3)

PALE CORYDALIS

Corydalis sempervirens (L.) Persoon

Named for the glaucous or pale character of the finely divided foliage, these perennial plants may reach 3 feet in height. The flowers are about ¾ inch long. A northern species that is infrequent to rare on open rocky slopes and outcrops in our mountains and a few piedmont counties.
April-May. (86-3-1)

Fumariaceae

YELLOW FUMEWORT

Corydalis micrantha ssp. *australis* (Chapm.) Ownbey

Rarely more than 1 foot high and with erect spikes of yellow flowers, plants of this species differ considerably from the larger ones described above.

A native of the central U.S. and a few of our mountain counties, this Fumewort appears to have been introduced in the Wilmington area where it is naturalized and spreading in the sandy soil of open roadsides and old fields. *March-April.* (86-3-3)

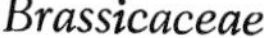

Brassicaceae

TOOTHWORT

Dentaria laciniata Willdenow

This native member of the Mustard family, sometimes included in the genus *Cardamine,* usually has 3 stem leaves deeply parted or divided into 5-9 segments 1-3 or more inches long. These plants, with flowers only ½ inch or less broad, are perennial from small, deeply set, fleshy tubers or jointed rhizomes.

A species of the eastern U.S. that is relatively frequent in the alluvial woods at scattered localities over the state, though it is most abundant in the mountains and piedmont. We have 3 other Toothworts in the state. *March-May.* (88-23-3)

Brassicaceae

BITTER CRESS

Cardamine clematitis Shuttleworth

Of our several native and introduced species of *Cardamine,* this one has the largest flowers with petals ¼ inch or more long. Plants of some species, as the common name implies, are used for cress, or salad.

This rhizomatous perennial is native only to the southern Appalachians and is found in North Carolina growing by, or in, rocky streams in the mountains. *April-May.* (88-23-7)

Sarraceniaceae

YELLOW PITCHER PLANT; TRUMPETS*

Sarracenia flava Linnaeus

Insects are trapped in the long, slender, hollow leaves of these interesting plants where they are digested and provide the plants with some of their mineral requirements; the leaves may be 12-36 inches tall. The flowers, with petals 2-3 inches or more long and a very strong musky scent, generally appear with or before the new leaves.

A native of the southeastern U.S. that is becoming quite rare on the savannahs and in the bogs and wet ditches of the coastal plain.

March-April. (89-1-1)

SWEET PITCHER PLANT*

Sarracenia rubra Walter

The flowering stems, generally from 8-18 inches tall, are nearly twice as long as the slender, hollow leaves. The flowers have the fragrance of violets and are smaller than those of our other species.

A rare, rhizomatous perennial of the southeastern U.S. still found in a few shrub bogs and savannahs of the coastal plain; it appears to be extinct at several previously known localities along mountain streams. The plant reaches its northern limit in our state. *April-May.* (89-1-2)

HOODED PITCHER PLANT*

Sarracenia minor Walter

The spotted, strongly hooded, hollow leaves of these plants, usually 6-12 inches tall, are about the same height as the stalk of the odorless flowers.

Another southeastern species that reaches its northern limit in North Carolina, these rhizomatous perennials are occasionally seen in the bogs, wet ditches, and savannahs of a few counties of our southeastern coastal plain. *April-May.* (89-1-3)

Sarraceniaceae

PITCHER PLANT; FLYTRAP*

Sarracenia purpurea Linnaeus

The open hollow leaves of plants of this species are 4-10 inches or more long and form a basal rosette around the flower stalk; they are often filled with water and decaying insects. The odorless flowers are about 2 inches broad and the petals about 2 inches long.

A now rare but once widespread species of the eastern U.S., these rhizomatous perennials are still found in a few bogs and moist savannahs of the coastal plain and at a few isolated localities in the mountains. *April-May.* (89-1-4)

Crassulaceae

MOSSY STONECROP

Sedum acre Linnaeus

A low, creeping perennial that forms evergreen mats. The fleshy leaves, less than ¼ inch long, are sharp pointed and strongly overlapped. The star-like flowers are about ¾ inch across.

An introduced plant, most common northward, that is naturalized in dry rocky areas of only 2 of our mountain counties. *May-June.* (91-1-3)

Crassulaceae

SEDUM; STONECROP

Sedum ternatum Michaux

The small, fleshy leaves of this prostrate perennial are rounded and in sets of 3. In these characters, as well as flower color, it differs from the previous species.

A native of the northeastern U.S. found scattered in rich, rocky but often moist woods of our piedmont and mountains. *April-June.* (91-1-5)

SEDUM; LIVE-FOR-EVER

Sedum telephioides Michaux

This is our most distinctive species of Sedum with wide, fleshy, petiolate leaves 1-2 inches long on an erect stem to 12 or more inches tall.

A species generally of the northern Appalachians, these plants grow in rock crevices and rocky woods of the North Carolina mountains and a few adjacent piedmont counties.
July-September. (91-1-9)

SUNDEW

Drosera intermedia Hayne

Flies and other small insects are caught by the shining, sticky droplets of mucilaginous material produced at the tips of the slender red hairs on the leaves of these diminutive plants. The small leaf blades are mostly ¼-½ inch long. The minute flowers stay open only a few hours.

Primarily a northern species, it is relatively frequent in our coastal plain, where it grows in standing water in bogs and wet ditches.

July-August. (92-1-4)

SUNDEW

Drosera rotundifolia Linnaeus

Although rather similar to the above species, the rounded leaf blades of these small plants are about as wide as long, thus the specific name. The glistening sticky droplet on each leaf hair accounts for the common name, Sundew.

These plants grow in the sphagnum bogs of a few of our mountain counties. Though rare in North Carolina, they are more common northward, their range extending from New England to Alaska. *July-September.* (92-1-3)

Dionaeaceae

VENUS' FLY TRAP*

Dionaea muscipula Ellis

This is one of the world's most unique plants. The 2-lobed leaf of these small native perennials is red inside and attracts flies and other insects that are then trapped when the 2 lobes, each about 1 inch long, suddenly close together. (See frontispiece)

A rare native perennial that is known only from the coastal area of the Carolinas, it is now extinct at many localities where it previously grew. It grows best in open sun either on low, wet sandy roadsides and ditch margins or on moist savannahs. *May-June.* *(93-1-1)*

Saxifragaceae

MOCK ORANGE

Philadelphus hirsutus Nuttall

A showy native shrub that may be 6 feet tall and is sometimes cultivated. The flowers are up to 1½ inches across, and the leaves, which are pubescent beneath, are usually 2-3 inches long.

A rare plant of the southern Appalachian region which is occasionally found on dry wooded bluffs and ledges in some of our mountain counties. *April-May.* *(94-4-2)*

Saxifragaceae

WILD HYDRANGEA

Hydrangea arborescens Linnaeus

The white, showy, 3-4 lobed calyx of the outer, sterile flowers is about ¾ inch across; the compact center of the inflorescence is made up of small fertile flowers. The under surface of the leaves of various subspecies of this spreading shrub may be white, gray, or green.

Native to the northern and central U.S., these shrubs grow on shady, often moist, roadbanks and cliffs of our mountains and upper piedmont. *May-July.* (94-5-1)

GRASS OF PARNASSUS

Parnassia asarifolia Ventenat

Three somewhat similar species of these low perennials occur in our area. The 5 petals with prominent green veins are up to ½ inch long in the species shown but somewhat shorter in our other species.

This species is native to the southern Appalachians and is rather rare in North Carolina, where it grows in bogs and on seepage slopes in the mountains. Another of the two additional species of *Parnassia* occurs in a few counties of the coastal plain. *August-October.* (94-6-1)

MITERWORT; FOAMFLOWER

Tiarella cordifolia Linnaeus

A rhizomatous perennial with roughly heart-shaped leaves 2-4 inches or more long. The flower stalks are 8-18 inches tall and bear a 1-3 inch long raceme. Older plants may form large clumps with many flower stalks.

These low herbs, native to the northeastern U.S. generally, are relatively frequent in the rich woods of our mountains and piedmont.

April-June. *(94-12-1)*

BROOK SAXIFRAGE

Boykinia aconitifolia Nuttall

A rhizomatous perennial with 2-5 inch wide leaves similar to those of *Aconitum* or Monkshood. The open inflorescence, composed of small flowers less than ¼ inch broad, is on a stalk usually 8-20 inches tall.

These plants are native to the Appalachian mountain region and are occasionally found along stream banks, in bogs, or on seepage slopes in a few of our western counties.

June-July. *(94-13-1)*

SAXIFRAGE

Saxifraga michauxii Britton

The coarsely serrate, obovate, or oblanceolate basal leaves are 2-4 inches or more long. The widely branched flower stalks of these perennials may be 4-20 inches tall; the flowers of this species are zygomorphic.

A species limited generally to the southern Appalachian region, these plants grow in the crevices of moist rocks and on seepage slopes in our mountains. *June-August.* *(94-14-1)*

MOUNTAIN LETTUCE

Saxifraga micranthidifolia (Haw.) Steudel

The regular corolla, the narrower inflorescence, and the larger, thinner leaves, some to nearly a foot long, help distinguish this species from the one above.

Another native perennial Saxifrage of the Appalachian area found infrequently in North Carolina, it too grows on moist rocks and seepage slopes in the mountains. *May-June.* *(94-14-4)*

WITCH-HAZEL

Hamamelis virginiana Linnaeus

A bushy shrub or small tree with toothed or shallowly lobed leaves 2-6 inches long. The leaves develop in the spring, while the blooms appear on naked branches in the fall or winter. The small flowers, with 4 linear petals about ½ inch long, are in compact clusters just above the old leaf scars. Witch Hazel extract is made from the dormant stems of the plant.

These plants are found in rich woods and along dry woodland margins throughout the state. Their general range is over the northeastern U.S., south to northern Georgia. *October-December.* (95-2-1)

WITCH ALDER; FOTHERGILLA

Fothergilla major (Sims) Loddiges

The compact spike of small, apetalous flowers with numerous white filaments is an inch or more long; the leaves are 3-5 inches long. A relatively rare colonial shrub, 3-6 feet tall, apparently limited to the dry woods of the piedmont and mountains of North Carolina and adjacent portions of Tennessee. A lower-growing species is found in our coastal plain.

April-May. (95-3-1)

WILD STRAWBERRY

Fragaria virginiana Duchesne

A low, native perennial often forming large colonies by means of stolons or "runners." The leaf is made up of 3 obovate, dentate leaflets each usually 1-2 inches long. The sweet, fleshy, red fruits are often more flavorsome than the related, but larger, cultivated strawberries.

A frequent to common plant of old fields and woodland borders throughout the state and much of the eastern U.S. *March-June.* *(97-1-1)*

MOCK STRAWBERRY; INDIAN STRAWBERRY

Duchesnea indica (Andr.) Focke

A low perennial with trifoliate leaves similar to those of the true strawberry but with yellow petals and a pulpy, tasteless fruit surrounded by 5 large toothed bracts. Note that Cinquefoil, the next species, has 5 leaflets and smaller bracts.

An introduced weed found in lawns, pastures, open woods, and on roadsides at scattered localities throughout our state and area.
February-October. *(97-2-1)*

CINQUEFOIL; FIVE FINGER

Potentilla canadensis Linnaeus

A rhizomatous perennial with 5 leaflets, the center one up to 1½ inches long. The young leaflets, petioles, and lower leaf surface are pubescent with long, silky hairs.

A northern species extending southward to Georgia, these often weedy plants are relatively frequent in pastures, lawns, and along the margins of woodlands more or less throughout our state. *March-May.* *(97-4-1)*

FLOWERING RASPBERRY; THIMBLEBERRY

Rubus odoratus Linnaeus

A bushy perennial with branched, bristly but not thorny, canes 3-6 feet tall. The attractive flowers are 1-2 inches broad and are followed by edible, but not very flavorsome, red raspberries.

Thimbleberry is native to the northeastern U.S. and extends into our area only in the mountains where they often grow in colonies or clumps on shady road banks, woodland borders, and along streams.
June-August. *(97-5-1)*

BLACKBERRY

Rubus argutus Link

One of the several white-flowered, thorny species of *Rubus* found in our area, with canes from 1-6 feet or more tall, these perennials often propagate by rhizomes, or runners, to form dense bramble thickets. The flowers are about 1 inch across; the juicy sweet black fruits are excellent when fully ripe.

Primarily a southeastern species that is often a weed in meadows, pastures, old fields, and woodland borders throughout North Carolina.

April-May. (97-5-9)

FALSE VIOLET; STAR VIOLET

Dalibarda repens Linnaeus

This low perennial with pubescent, creeping stems has leaves 1-2 inches long that resemble those of some violets, which accounts for the common name. The flowers are about ½ inch across.

North Carolina is the southern limit of this more northern species, our rarest member of the Rose family. It is known from mossy bogs in only a single mountain county. *June-September.* (97-6-1)

AVENS; GEUM

Geum radiatum Gray

There are seven species of *Geum* in North Carolina with yellow, white, or pink petals, but only this one has large flowers nearly 1½ inches across.

These rare native perennials are known only from the high balds in our northwest mountains and a few adjacent areas of Tennessee; another yellow flowered species, *G. virginianum,* is more widespread.

June-August. (97-7-7)

CANADA BURNET

Sanguisorba canadensis Linnaeus

Although the small flowers have no petals, their showy stamens and compact arrangement produce a conspicuous inflorescence 3-6 inches or more long on stems 2-5 feet tall. The large, basal, pinnate leaves have 7-15 serrate leaflets.

These native perennials are infrequent to rare in the mountain bogs and wet meadows of some of our western counties, where they are near the southern limit of the range for this species.

July-September. (97-10-3)

Rosaceae

SWAMP ROSE

Rosa palustris Marshall

These rhizomatous perennials, with thorny, upright canes to 6 feet long, have pinnately compound leaves with 5-9 elliptic leaflets usually 1-2 inches long. The flowers are about 2 inches across.

A native of the eastern U.S. that is scattered but relatively frequent along the margins of streams, ponds, or swamp forests essentially throughout our state. *May-July.* *(97-11-11)*

INDIAN-PHYSIC; FAWN'S BREATH

Gillenia trifoliata (L.) Moench

The 3 leaflets and the 5 linear, slightly twisted, and unequal petals help identify this open, branching perennial that grows to a height of 2-3 feet. The roots are purgative.

A native found primarily in the Atlantic Coast states from our area northward, *Gillenia* grows in the rich woods of the North Carolina mountains and northern piedmont.
April-June. *(97-13-1)*

Rosaceae

GOAT'S BEARD

Aruncus dioicus (Walt.) Fernald

As the species name implies, these tall perennials with large bipinnately or tripinnately compound leaves are dioecious, having the male and female flowers on separate plants; the male plant is shown here. The ovate to lanceolate, serrate leaflets may be 2-5 inches long.

A species of the northern and central U.S. found growing in the rich, moist woods of our mountains and piedmont. *May-June.* (97-14-1)

HARDHACK; SPIRAEA

Spiraea tomentosa Linnaeus

The leaves of these perennial shrubs are simple, tomentose beneath, elliptic to ovate, and 1-2 inches long. The flowers at the top of the inflorescence open first.

Though occasionally found in wet meadows or low woodland borders at scattered localities over most of the western and northern portions of the state, these plants are more common northward.

July-September. (97-15-2)

NINEBARK

Physocarpus opulifolius (L.) Maximowicz

A shrub 3-6 feet or more tall with simple leaves and thin, separating layers of old bark on the larger stems. The cluster of flowers is about 2 inches broad. A native of the northeastern U.S. that is sometimes cultivated, these shrubs grow along stream banks and on moist cliffs in our mountains and piedmont. *May-July.* *(97-16-1)*

CRAB APPLE

Malus angustifolia (Ait.) Michaux

The delicate, fragrant flowers of this small tree or shrub are about ¾ inch across. The pink petals soon fade to almost white. The hard, green, extremely sour apples are rich in pectin and are used in jelly. A southeastern species found growing along fencerows and low woodland margins chiefly of our coastal plain and mountains. *April-May.* (97-18-2)

MOUNTAIN ASH

Sorbus americana Marshall

The large, dark green, pinnate leaves and the compact clusters of white flowers or bright red fruits identify this striking small tree. A northern species that may be found growing around rock outcrops, balds, and the margins of spruce-fir forests at high elevations in our mountains.

June-July. (97-19-1)

RED CHOKEBERRY

Sorbus arbutifolia (L.) Heynhold

Usually a low shrub 1-5 feet tall with simple, alternate leaves. The flowers are about ¼ inch across and are in clusters at or near the ends of the short branches; the bright red, apple-like fruits are only ¼ inch in diameter.

A species of the eastern U.S. that is frequent in bogs, savannahs, and low woodlands throughout the state.

March-May. (97-19-2)

Rosaceae

HAWTHORN

Crataegus flabellata (Bosc) K. Koch

This tall shrub, with serrate, roughly heart-shaped leaves 2-3 inches wide and clusters of ½ inch broad flowers, is so variable and so poorly understood that over a dozen species and varieties have been described from the plants here considered to be a single species. Native to the northeastern U.S., Hawthorns are found throughout our area in woodlands, pastures, and thickets. *May-June.* (97-20-4)

SHADBUSH; SERVICEBERRY

Amelanchier arborea (Michx. f.) Fernald

A shrub or small tree with drooping racemes of white or pale pink flowers followed by small, reddish purple, apple-like fruits. The petals are about ½ inch long. Native to the eastern U.S., these plants grow in open, often rocky, woodlands chiefly in our mountains and piedmont. *March-May.* (97-21-1)

Rosaceae

WILD CHERRY; BLACK CHERRY

Prunus serotina Ehrhart

The leaves of this native tree are mostly 2-3 inches long and are poisonous when wilted. The small flowers are ¼ inch, or slightly more, across. The juicy, dark reddish black fruits are about ¼ inch in diameter and may be sweet or bitter. A species of the eastern U.S. that is found in low woodlands and along fencerows throughout the state. *April-May.* (97-22-11)

Fabaceae

SENSITIVE BRIER

Schrankia microphylla (Smith) Macbride

The bipinnately compound leaves of this thorny, sprawling vine close at the slightest touch. The globose cluster of many small flowers is about ½ inch in diameter. A southeastern species found along clay roadsides and woodland margins in all provinces, but rare or absent from the outer coastal plain. *June-September.* (98-2-1)

REDBUD; JUDAS TREE*

Cercis canadensis Linnaeus

A small, fast-growing, often cultivated tree with black bark and simple, heart-shaped leaves that appear after the period of profuse flowering. The numerous small flowers are soon followed by flat, oblong pods 2-3 inches long.

These native southeastern trees grow in cut-over woodlands and along fencerows, especially on sweet or basic soils, chiefly in our piedmont.
March-May. *(98-4-1)*

PARTRIDGE PEA; SENNA

Cassia fasciculata Michaux

These herbaceous annuals are 6-36 inches tall. The flowers, which are an inch or more broad, are not as strongly zygomorphic as the flowers of most legumes although the 5 petals do differ considerably in size.

A native of the eastern and central U.S., these weedy plants frequently grow in old fields and along roadsides and forest margins throughout the state. *June-September.* *(98-5-5)*

YELLOWWOOD

Cladrastis lutea (Michx. f.) K. Koch

The showy racemes of this native tree are 8-24 inches or more long. The gray or light brown bark of the trunk is smooth; the wood is yellow and has been used as a source of dye.

This tree of the Appalachian area is found in the rich woods of only a few of our mountain counties. It is often planted elsewhere as an ornamental. *April-May.* *(98-8-1)*

FALSE INDIGO

Baptisia australis (L.) R. Brown

These plants, with flowers an inch long, may reach a height of 3 feet. The thick, short pods are black. The flowers and leaves characteristic of many leguminous plants are well illustrated in this picture.

Although native to the mid-area of the eastern U.S., these perennials, widely planted as ornamentals, grow in open woods and clearings on basic soil in a few counties in our northern piedmont. *April-August.* *(98-9-2)*

BUSH PEA*

Thermopsis villosa (Walt.) Fernald & Schubert

A close relative of *Baptisia,* these native perennials may grow to 3 feet or more in height. The pods, or legumes, of this species are villous, or densely pubescent with long hairs.

These plants, with a general range throughout the southern Appalachian region, grow in clearings or along forest margins in a few of our western counties. *May-June.* *(98-10-1)*

INDIGO BUSH

Amorpha fruticosa Linnaeus

A native shrub, up to 12 feet or more in height, that has alternate, pinnately compound leaves that vary considerably as to leaflet number and shape. The erect racemes of small flowers are often 8-20 inches long. These plants range over much of the eastern U.S. and grow along stream banks and in open woods at scattered localities in all provinces of North Carolina. *April-May.* (98-18-5)

BLACK LOCUST

Robinia pseudo-acacia Linnaeus

Widely planted as an ornamental, these thorny, native trees have attractive, drooping racemes, 4-8 inches long. The very fragrant flowers are about ¾ inch long. The wood makes durable fence posts and pilings.

A native of the southeastern U.S., this sometimes weedy tree grows in old fields or along roadsides, fencerows, and woodland margins, chiefly in our piedmont and mountains. *April-June.* (98-32-1)

BRISTLY LOCUST

Robinia hispida Linnaeus

This attractive shrub, usually 2-8 feet tall, often forms large colonies by stolons. The leaflets of the pinnately compound leaf are 1-2 inches long and the attractive, inodorus flowers are about 1 inch long.

A species native to the southeast that is found along road banks and woodland margins at scattered localities in all provinces of North Carolina. *May-June.* (98-32-4)

Fabaceae

GOAT'S RUE

Tephrosia virginiana (L.) Persoon

A low, villous, native perennial with unbranched stems 8-20 inches tall terminating in an open inflorescence. The large white top petal, about ½ inch across, is the "standard," the pink lateral petals are the "wings," and the two fused lower petals the "keel" of this typical pea flower.

A relatively frequent plant along the margins of woodlands or in open woods more or less throughout the state and eastern U.S.

May-June. (98-34-1)

BUTTERFLY PEA

Clitoria mariana Linnaeus

A slender, twining or trailing perennial vine with trifoliolate leaves and large, conspicuous flowers that have a standard 1 inch or more long or wide.

A southern native that is found essentially throughout our area growing in open, usually dry, woods and clearings. *June-August.* (98-42-1)

Oxalidaceae

WOOD SORREL; WOOD SHAMROCK

Oxalis acetosella Linnaeus

The leaves and the 3-4 inch tall flowering stems arise directly from a creeping rhizome. The heart-shaped leaflets may be an inch or more wide, and the flower is about an inch across.

North Carolina is near the southern limit for these plants that grow in cool moist forests, often under hemlock or spruce trees, at high elevations in our western counties. *May-September.* (100-1-1)

PINK WOOD SORREL

Oxalis violacea Linnaeus

Each leafless flower stalk of these low plants bears several pink (not violet) flowers about ¾ inch across. They arise from small bulbs and not from rhizomes as is the case with the species described above.

A perennial native to much of the eastern U.S. which is found in alluvial woods or rich upland woods at numerous scattered localities across North Carolina. *April-May.* (100-1-3)

Oxalidaceae

SOURGRASS; OXALIS

Oxalis grandis Small

This is the largest of about half a dozen yellow-flowered species of *Oxalis* in our area. The plants may be 1-2 feet tall and the leaflets, edged with a thin maroon line, are 1-2 inches wide.

A more northern species that is found in North Carolina in the rich woods of the mountains and, less frequently, the upper piedmont. *May-June.* (100-1-8)

Geraniaceae

WILD GERANIUM

Geranium maculatum Linnaeus

This erect, rhizomatous perennial grows to a height of 12-24 inches. The largest of the deeply cleft leaves are 2-4 inches wide, and the flowers may be 1 inch or more across.

Native to the eastern U.S., these plants grow in alluvial woods and in rich coves chiefly in our mountains and piedmont. *April-June.* (101-1-1)

FRINGED POLYGALA; GAY WINGS

Polygala paucifolia Willdenow

The few leaves of this 3-4 inch tall, rhizomatous perennial are crowded near the top of the stem. The colorful flowers, the largest found in any of our Polygalas, are nearly an inch long.

A plant of the northeastern U.S. that grows in the deciduous forests at high elevations in a few western North Carolina counties, where it is near the southern limit of its range. *April-June.* (106-1-1)

POLYGALA

Polygala curtissii Gray

A slender, branched, native annual, 4-8 inches or more tall. The numerous small flowers, each about ¼ inch long, are borne in compact racemes at the ends of short terminal branches that continue to develop and produce buds over a long season.

These plants grow in old fields and along moist woodland borders at many scattered localities in the piedmont and mountains of North Carolina. Their general range is the southeastern U.S. *June-October.* (106-1-7)

Polygalaceae

YELLOW MILKWORT

Polygala lutea Linnaeus

This native biennial is our most colorful species of *Polygala* and sometimes grows to a height of a foot or more. The compact racemes, about ¾ inch in diameter, continue to grow and produce flower buds throughout the summer; the small fruits fall when ripe leaving scars on the flower stalk beneath the current blooms.

A southeastern species that is fairly common on roadsides, savannahs, and in pine barrens throughout our coastal plain. *April-October.* *(106-1-14)*

Euphorbiaceae

STINGING NETTLE

Cnidoscolus stimulosus

(Michx.) Engelmann & Gray

These low, monoecious, perennial herbs are armed with numerous stinging hairs. The fragrant flowers have no petals, but the 5-lobed calyx, about ½ inch broad, is white and petaloid.

A native of the southeastern coastal plain, these plants are relatively frequent in the sandhills and old sandy fields of eastern North Carolina. *March-August.* *(107-1-1)*

CROTON

Croton punctatus Jacquin

A rather coarse, branched, monoecious, perennial herb to 3 feet tall which is profusely dotted with small scales and glands that give the entire plant a brownish gray cast. The small, inconspicuous female flowers produce 3-lobed capsules that may attain a width of ½ inch.

These plants grow only on, or just behind, the sand dunes along the coast reaching their northern limit in Dare County.

May-November. (107-2-2)

POINSETTIA; PAINTED LEAF

Euphorbia heterophylla Linnaeus

The wild relative of our colorful cultivated Poinsettias, these small annuals have upper leaves 2-3 inches long which vary in color, pattern, and shape just below the inflorescence of small inconspicuous flowers.

A semi-weedy plant of the Gulf and South Atlantic coastal plains as far north as Virginia, the species is known from disturbed habitats in seven of our eastern counties. *June-October.* (107-11-2)

Euphorbiaceae

CAROLINA IPECAC

Euphorbia ipecacuanhae Linnaeus

These low, exceptionally variable, monoecious, deep-rooted herbs usually form dark green tufts or small mats. The minute female flowers produce small, 3-lobed capsules characteristic of the Spurge family.

Another plant of the southeastern U.S. coastal plain, these perennials, once used medicinally as an emetic, grow in the sandy pinelands and turkey-oak woods of eastern North Carolina. *March-May.* *(107-11-10)*

MILKWEED; FLOWERING SPURGE

Euphorbia corollata Linnaeus

The sap of these slender, branched, 1-3 foot tall perennials is milky, which is a characteristic of most members of this family. The numerous flowers, about ¼ inch broad, lack petals and sepals but have 5 showy, white petaloid glands that attract pollinators.

A widespread species of the eastern U.S. that grows in old fields, clearings, and waste places throughout most of North Carolina except the outer coastal plain. *May-September.* *(107-11-13)*

POISON SUMAC; THUNDERWOOD

Rhus vernix Linnaeus

A shrub or small tree 6-20 feet tall with smooth, light gray bark and pinnately compound leaves that are especially colorful in the fall. It produces a contact skin poison that may prove extremely severe, or even fatal, to many people. The plant has small green flowers in an axillary inflorescence and small, globose, white fruits. Native to the eastern U.S., this shrub grows in bogs, swamp margins, bays, and wet pine barrens of our mountains and coastal plain. *May-June.* *(110-1-1)*

SMOOTH SUMAC

Rhus glabra Linnaeus

A non-toxic shrub or small tree with more numerous and more slender leaflets than Poison Sumac, and a compact, terminal cluster of small, red fruits.

Widespread over the eastern and central U.S., Smooth Sumac grows in dry soils of old fields, along woodland borders and in waste places in our mountains, piedmont, and inner coastal plain. *Late May-July.* *(110-1-8)*

Anacardiaceae

POISON IVY

Rhus radicans Linnaeus

Direct or indirect contact with any part of these poisonous woody vines results in severe inflamation and blistering of the skin of many people. However, the three smooth, acuminate leaflets, each usually 2-4 inches long are easy to recognize. The three leaflets of the related Poison Oak, usually a low shrub and not a vine, are lobed and more rounded but equally toxic.

Native over the eastern U.S., this common plant grows by roadsides, by fencerows, in low woodlands, and in waste places throughout the state. *April-May.* *(110-1-2)*

Vitaceae

VIRGINIA CREEPER; WOODVINE

Parthenocissus quinquefolia (L.) Planchon

This harmless, often cultivated woody vine is a member of the Grape family and is taken out of sequence in order to afford a comparison with Poison Ivy, with which it is often confused. The 5 leaflets, each 2-6 inches or more long, are distinctive in both shape and number.

A native of eastern U.S. that is common in dry or rich woods, on sand dunes, and often in waste places throughout the state. *May-July.* *(120-1-1)*

HOLLY; AMERICAN HOLLY

Ilex opaca Aiton

A slow-growing, evergreen tree with smooth, gray-green bark and leathery, spiny leaves that are mostly 2-3 inches long. The trees are dioecious, thus the colorful red berries, about ¼ inch in diameter, occur only on the trees that produce the small white female (pistillate) flowers.

These native trees grow scattered in deciduous woods throughout North Carolina and the eastern U.S. *April-June.* (112-1-1)

MOUNTAIN HOLLY

Ilex montana Torrey & Gray

A dioecious native shrub or small tree with berries ¼ inch or more in diameter on the female plants. The thin, deciduous leaves are 2-6 inches long.

These plants, native to the northeastern U.S., grow in mixed hardwood and pine woodlands chiefly in our mountains and piedmont. *April-June.* (112-1-6)

STRAWBERRY BUSH; HEARTS A'BUSTIN

Euonymus americanus Linnaeus

These slender, upright or trailing, shrubs grow 3-6 feet tall and have smooth green stems, thick, opposite leaves and inconspicuous, flat, greenish cream flowers about ½ inch across. The warty red fruits, 1-2 inches across, open in the early fall exposing the crimson seeds.

A southern species that occurs north to Pennsylvania, these plants are relatively frequent in the mixed deciduous forests and low woodlands throughout our area. *May-June.* (113-3-2)

Aceraceae

MOUNTAIN MAPLE

Acer spicatum Lamarck

A monoecious shrub or small, bushy tree that has slender panicles of greenish white flowers in erect, terminal racemes. The opposite leaves are usually 3-lobed, sharply toothed, and 3-5 inches long or wide. The winged fruits are red when young but turn brown when ripe.

A native of the northeastern U.S., these trees grow in clumps in the rich, rocky woods at elevations above 4,000 feet in our mountains. *May-July.* (115-1-2)

Hippocastanaceae

RED BUCKEYE

Aesculus pavia Linnaeus

A low shrub or rarely a small tree that is easily recognized when in bloom by the large, open cluster of 1 inch long red flowers. The leaves are palmately compound with 5 slender leaflets usually 1-2 inches wide. These natives of the southeast, sometimes cultivated, are occasionally found in the low woodlands and along swamp margins in our southern coastal plain counties. *April-May.* (116-1-2)

Hippocastanaceae

BUCKEYE

Aesculus octandra Marshall

A shrub or small tree with opposite, palmately compound leaves and yellowish green flowers about an inch long. The large, rounded brown seeds or "Buckeyes" are poisonous. This more northern species occurs in the rich cove forests and deciduous woodlands of our mountains. A bushy species, *A. sylvatica,* occurs in much of the piedmont. *May.* (116-1-3)

Balsaminaceae

PALE JEWEL WEED

Impatiens pallida Nuttall

A branched, succulent-stemmed, native annual herb 2-6 feet tall with spurred, zygomorphic, weakly spotted flowers about an inch long.

A plant of the northeastern U.S. that grows in moist areas with neutral or basic soil, it is found in the mountains and a few piedmont counties in North Carolina. *July-September.* (118-1-1)

JEWEL WEED

Impatiens capensis Meerburgh

A native annual herb very similar to the previous species except for flower color and, usually, a difference in habitat.

These plants grow in moist open areas along streams and in low woods in acid soils throughout most of North Carolina and the eastern U.S. *May-frost.* (118-1-2)

Rhamnaceae

NEW JERSEY TEA

Ceanothus americanus Linnaeus

A low bushy shrub 1-3 feet tall with terminal clusters of numerous small flowers. The leaves, which at one time were dried and used as a tea substitute, are alternate, mostly 2-3 inches long, and pubescent to pilose beneath.

These shrubs are relatively frequent in open woodlands, on forest margins, and along roadsides throughout our state and much of the eastern U.S. *May-June.* *(119-2-1)*

Malvaceae

FLOWER-OF-AN-HOUR

Hibiscus trionum Linnaeus

As the common name implies, the attractive 1½ inch broad flower of these low, hairy, annual herbs lasts but a short time. The calyx becomes inflated to form a papery "pod" around the maturing fruit.

These introduced Mallows occasionally grow in cultivated fields and along sandy roadsides chiefly in our coastal plain and piedmont. *June-October.* *(122-8-5)*

Malvaceae

SWAMP MALLOW

Hibiscus moscheutos Linnaeus

The conspicuous flowers of these shrubby perennial herbs are 4-6 inches across; the numerous anthers are united into a column around the style, a characteristic of the Mallow family. The lanceolate leaves of Swamp Mallow are 4-6 inches or more long.

A native of the southeastern U.S. that occurs in the coastal plain and piedmont of North Carolina where the plants grow along the edges of marshes and swamp forests. *June-September.* (122-8-2)

Theaceae

SILKY CAMELLIA; STEWARTIA*

Stewartia malacodendron Linnaeus

This member of the Tea Family is one of our most beautiful and rarest, native shrubs. The camellia-like flowers are 2-3 inches across.

These primarily southeastern plants grow in low woodlands and along creek banks chiefly in our coastal plain but also at a few scattered localities in the piedmont and mountains. *May-June.* (124-1-1)

Theaceae

LOBLOLLY BAY

Gordonia lasianthus (L.) Ellis

The thick, glossy evergreen leaves of this shrub or small tree are often ragged where chewed by insects. The camellia-like flowers are about 2 inches across; the round, pubescent buds are about ½ inch in diameter. These plants grow in the bay forests and in thickets along low ditches in the coastal plain of North Carolina where they reach their northern limit. *July-August.* *(124-2-1)*

Hypericaceae

ST. JOHN'S WORT

Hypericum prolificum Linnaeus

These coarse shrubs are up to 5 feet or more tall, yet the numerous, slender stamens give a light feathery appearance to the clustered, 1 inch broad, showy flowers. A species of the northeastern U.S., it is native in our mountains and piedmont where it grows in meadows and seepage slopes at scattered localities. *June-August.* *(126-1-8)*

Hypericaceae

HYPERICUM

Hypericum buckleyi M. A. Curtis

Our 20 or more yellow-flowered *Hypericum* species can be recognized as a group by their generally similar flower structure and leaves dotted with minute glands.

This species, native only to the southern Appalachians, grows on the balds, seepage slopes, and in rock crevices of our mountains. *June-August.* (126-1-15)

Cistaceae

HUDSONIA

Hudsonia montana Nuttall

A very rare small shrub with solitary flowers, about 1 inch wide, at the ends of short branches. The linear leaves are spreading and thus differ from the leaves closely appressed to the stem in *Hudsonia tomentosa* of our coastal plain. This endemic plant is known only from shrub balds in a single mountain county. *June-July.* (129-1-2)

BIRDFOOT VIOLET*

Viola pedata Linnaeus

A small, rhizomatous Violet with 1 inch broad flowers that are usually lavender, rarely white, or occasionally bicolored, in which case the upper 2 petals are deep purple and the 3 lower ones lavender.

These plants, native of the eastern U.S., grow in rocky, open woodlands and on clay roadsides throughout the mountains and piedmont as well as in many of our coastal plain counties. *March-May.* (130-2-1)

HAIRY VIOLET

Viola villosa Walter

These small, rhizomatous perennials, like most other violets, bear 2 kinds of flowers: open, cross-pollinated flowers with colorful petals; and closed, self-pollinated flowers that do not develop petals.

These rare native plants of the southeastern U.S., only 1-2 inches tall, grow in moist, sandy or rocky soil at the margins of pocosins and woodlands in a few scattered localities in all provinces. *February-April.* (130-2-6)

LANCE-LEAVED VIOLET

Viola lanceotata Linnaeus

The erect, or suberect, toothed, lanceolate leaves of these small, stoloniferous, perennials are usually 1-3 inches long. The flowers are about ¼ inch across.

Although this native of the eastern U.S. is found chiefly on the coastal plain, the quite similar and closely related *V. primulifolia* is found in similar moist habitats throughout the state.

March-May. *(130-2-16)*

HALBERD-LEAVED YELLOW VIOLET

Viola hastata Michaux

Each year these low, rhizomatous perennials produce only 2 or 3 leaves, distinctive in shape and coloration, which are 1-2 inches wide at the base. In North Carolina these natives of the southeastern U.S. grow in usually moist, deciduous woods of the mountains and piedmont.

March-May. *(130-2-19)*

Violaceae

LONG-SPURRED VIOLET

Viola rostrata Pursh

The flower of this rhizomatous, perennial Violet has a slender spur ½ inch or more long (here seen just under the curve in the flower stalk).

A native of the northeastern U.S., these plants are infrequent in our area where they grow in moist woods and hemlock forests in a few of our mountain counties. *April-May.* (130-2-23)

FIELD PANSY

Viola rafinesquii Greene

Of our more than 20 Violet species, this is one of the few annuals. The flowers are usually ¼ inch or less broad.

Although rather widespread in pastures, lawns, and along roadsides in the eastern U.S., and frequent in our mountains and piedmont, there is some question as to whether these small, attractive weeds are native. *March-May.* (130-2-28)

Passifloraceae

PASSION FLOWER; MAYPOPS

Passiflora incarnata Linnaeus

The intricate flowers of this herbaceous, trailing vine are 2-3 inches in diameter. The small, melon-shaped, edible fruits are 1-2 inches long, and "pop" if mashed. These native perennials of the southeastern U.S. are found in every county of North Carolina growing in fields and along roadsides and fencerows. *May-July.* *(131-1-1)*

Cactaceae

CACTUS; PRICKLY PEAR

Opuntia compressa (Salisb.) Macbride

The flattened, fleshy, green stems of this perennial are jointed, each joint, or "pad," is 2-4 inches or more broad and bears small clusters of numerous fine spines. The peeled fruit is edible.

These plants are primarily northeastern in distribution but also grow in dry, sandy or rocky habitats at scattered localities throughout North Carolina. *May-June.* *(132-1-1)*

Melastomataceae

MEADOW BEAUTY

Rhexia virginica Linnaeus

These perennials, usually 8-24 inches tall, have pubescent, winged stems. The flowers, which last for only a few hours, are about 1 inch across.

There are 8 species of these southeastern plants native to our area in bogs, ditches, and low meadows. The flowers may be rose-white, red-purple, or yellow. Plants of this species are native chiefly to the mountains and inner coastal plain.

May-September. *(136-1-7)*

Onagraceae

LUDWIGIA

Ludwigia bonariensis (Micheli) Hara

This tall, branched, perennial herb has conspicuous 4-petaled flowers 1-2 inches across that are similar to those of the closely related Evening Primrose. These plants, introduced from South America, are thoroughly naturalized in the marshes and low ditches of the Wilmington area.

June-September. *(137-1-2)*

EVENING PRIMROSE

Oenothera biennis Linnaeus

A rather coarse, variable, biennial, usually 8-30 inches tall, with lanceolate leaves and terminal clusters of slender, conical buds opening into showy yellow flowers 1-2 inches across.

Native throughout the eastern U.S., these somewhat weedy plants are frequent or common in old fields and along roadsides throughout the state.

June-October. (137-2-1)

SUNDROPS

Oenothera tetragona Roth

These perennials, with flowers an inch or more across, appear to hybridize with other similar species and therefore are quite variable.

Natives of the eastern U.S., they are found chiefly in the mountain areas of North Carolina where they grow in open woods, in meadows, and along roadsides.

May-August. (137-2-10)

Onagraceae

FIREWEED

Epilobium angustifolium Linnaeus

The slender stems of these native perennials may be up to 5 feet tall, with numerous, alternate, lanceolate leaves below the elongate inflorescence. The flowers are about 1½ inches across.

A northern species with a transcontinental range, these plants grow in recently cleared or burned areas. They are found only at high elevations in a few of our mountain counties.

July-September. *(137-3-2)*

Araliaceae

GINSENG; SANG*

Panax quinquefolium Linnaeus

Because the dried root of this perennial herb was once valuable in Chinese folk medicine, the plants, usually 8-20 inches tall, have almost been exterminated. The 3-5 stalked leaflets and small red fruits, about ¼ inch in diameter, are characteristic of this species. A native of the eastern U.S., these plants are now rare in the rich woods of our mountains and piedmont.

May-June. *(139-2-2)*

DWARF GINSENG

Panax trifolium Linnaeus

A close relative of Ginseng, these small perennials, 3-8 inches tall, have 3 sessile leaflets per leaf and fruits more yellow than red; the roots are globose rather than elongate and are without commercial value.

These plants grow in rich woods and are very rare in our area, which is at the southern limit of their more northern range, being known to grow in only 3 counties in North Carolina.

April-June. (139-2-1)

SPIKENARD

Aralia racemosa Linnaeus

This thornless, herbaceous perennial may grow to a height of 8 feet and has a large, aromatic root. The clusters of small, greenish white flowers are borne in long, compound racemes. The 3-7 leaflets may be 3-8 inches long.

Spikenard is relatively infrequent in the rich woods of our mountain counties where it is near the southern limit of its range.

June-August. (139-3-3)

Apiaceae

MARSH PENNYWORT

Hydrocotyle umbellata Linnaeus

The round, peltate, succulent, dark green leaves and the flower stalks arise from elongate rhizomes. The small flowers are in a compact umbel that is usually ¼-½ inch in diameter. Native to much of the eastern U.S., these mat-forming perennials commonly grow in moist, open areas and in roadside ditches of our coastal plain. *April-September.* (140-1-1)

WILD CARROT; QUEEN ANNE'S LACE

Daucus carota Linnaeus

The attractive, 2-4 inch "flower" is actually a compound inflorescence made up of many small flowers.

A common, introduced, biennial weed, 1-4 feet tall, that is found in fallow fields, waste places, and along roadsides throughout North Carolina and much of the eastern U.S. *May-September.* (140-5-1)

Apiaceae

MEADOW PARSNIP; GOLDEN ALEXANDER

Zizia trifoliata (Michx.) Fernald

The compound umbel of this aromatic perennial is 1-2 inches broad and consists of many small, 5-petaled flowers. Three yellow-flowered species of *Zizia* and 2 of the closely related *Thaspium* occur in our area. This Appalachian species grows in open woodlands, forest margins, and on roadsides in our mountains and piedmont. *April-May.* *(140-14-3)*

Cornaceae

FLOWERING DOGWOOD*

Cornus florida Linnaeus

The state flower of North Carolina and the state tree of several other southeastern states, it bears clusters of small, inconspicuous, greenish yellow flowers with 4 subtending, white, 2-3 inch long bracts that function as showy petals. Clusters of brilliant red berries form in the fall. These small native trees are frequent to common in open woodlands throughout the state and over much of the eastern U.S. *March-April.* *(142-1-1)*

Cornaceae

BUSH DOGWOOD

Cornus amomum Miller

A native, opposite-leaved shrub, often 4-8 feet or more tall, with 2-3 inch broad clusters of small white flowers followed in the fall by small blue, or bluish white, fruits.

A northeastern species found along swamp borders and in the marshes and alluvial woods chiefly of our mountains and piedmont.

June. *(142-1-3)*

Clethraceae

WHITE ALDER; SWEET PEPPER BUSH

Clethra acuminata Michaux

A native shrub or small tree with thin leaves 3-5 inches long and slender simple racemes. Our coastal plain species, *Clethra alnifolia,* has leaves 1-3 inches long and simple or compound racemes of very fragrant flowers.

This species is native to the Appalachian region and occurs sporadically in rich, moist woods of our high mountains.

June-July. *(143-1-1)*

INDIAN PIPES

Monotropa uniflora Linnaeus

These pale, low, fleshy, saprophytic perennials, sometimes mistaken for fungi, are in the same family as *Rhododendron*. The nodding flowers, about ¾ inch long, are basically similar to those of other members of the Heath family. The stems straighten so that the capsule is erect.

A northern and eastern species found in deciduous woods at scattered localities throughout our state.

June-October. (145-3-1)

PINESAP

Monotropa hypopithys Linnaeus

Plants of this species, like those of Indian Pipes, are also saprophytes, growing on decaying wood buried in the soil or leaf mold. However, the smaller and more numerous flowers and the tawny yellow to red coloration make separation of the 2 species easy.

A northern species that grows in deciduous woodlands at scattered localities more or less throughout North Carolina.

May-October. (145-3-2)

ROSEBAY; GREAT LAUREL*

Rhododendron maximum Linnaeus

A large shrub or sometimes a small tree with leathery, evergreen leaves 4-10 inches long and large clusters of pale pink flowers that are 1½ inches or more across. The shrubs alternate a year of bloom with a year of growth.

Primarily of Appalachian distribution, these plants grow along streams in cool forests in our lower mountains and the piedmont.
June-July. (145-5-1)

PURPLE LAUREL; RHODODENDRON*

Rhododendron catawbiense Michaux

A handsome, often cultivated, shrub or small tree with darker, rose-lavender flowers and leaves, mostly 3-6 inches long, generally shorter than in the preceding species. Frequent, often in large stands, on the higher rocky slopes, ridges, and balds in our mountains and piedmont; their general range is the Appalachian region. *April-June.* (145-5-2)

Ericaceae

PINKSHELL AZALEA*

Rhododendron vaseyi Gray

The bright pink flowers, with slender, exserted stamens and a style 1 inch or more long, open before the leaves come out on these rare shrubs.

Native only to North Carolina, but cultivated elsewhere, these tall shrubs grow infrequently in bogs and in spruce forests at high elevations in 3 of our mountain counties. *May-June.* (145-5-4)

FLAME AZALEA*

Rhododendron calendulaceum (Michx.) Torrey

Probably the most widely cultivated of our Azaleas, these native shrubs have flowers an inch or more across of varying shades of orange or yellow and add brilliant splashes of color to the spring forests.

Another native Appalachian species, these plants grow in the deciduous forests and on forest margins in our mountains. *May-June.* (145-5-5)

PINXTER-FLOWER*

Rhododendron nudiflorum (L.) Torrey

The almost odorless flowers, about 1 inch across, usually appear on these shrubs before the thin elliptic leaves.

A northeastern species, these plants are relatively frequent, though widely scattered, along streams in the deciduous forests and in low woodlands more or less throughout our state. *March-May.* *(145-5-9)*

DWARF AZALEA*

Rhododendron atlanticum (Ashe) Rehder

Rarely over 18 inches tall, these stoloniferous, weakly branched shrubs often form large colonies. The fragrant white flowers, 1-2 inches long, appear before the leaves. A coastal species found from New Jersey to Georgia, these shrubs are frequent to common along woodland borders, on savannahs, and in low, moist areas throughout our coastal plain.
April-May. *(145-5-10)*

Ericaceae

CLAMMY HONEYSUCKLE*

Rhododendron viscosum (L.) Torrey

A large, branched, native shrub to 8 feet or more tall with glandular-pubescent, sticky or clammy leaves that are well developed at flowering time. The long slender tube of the fragrant flower is an inch or more long.

Although of generally northeastern distribution, these plants grow on the borders of streams, ponds, and bogs at numerous scattered localities essentially throughout North Carolina. *May-July.* *(145-5-11)*

SAND MYRTLE*

Leiophyllum buxifolium (Berg.) Elliott

This is an evergreen shrub, sometimes low and spreading in the mountains and usually rather tall and erect in the coastal plain, with smooth, shiny leaves ¼-½ inch long.

Primarily a coastal plain species found from New Jersey to South Carolina in sandy woods; a near prostrate variety grows in dry, rocky areas in a few counties of our piedmont and mountains.

March-May. *(145-7-1)*

Ericaceae

IVY; MOUNTAIN LAUREL*

Kalmia latifolia Linnaeus

The leathery, evergreen, alternate leaves of this shrub are elliptical and mostly 2-3 inches long. The corolla, of 5 fused petals, is about ½ inch broad. A northeastern species of balds and deciduous woods that is frequent or common in our mountains and infrequent to rare in the piedmont and inner coastal plain. *April-June.* (145-8-1)

SHEEP LAUREL; WICKY

Kalmia angustifolia var. *caroliniana* (Small) Fernald

The leaves of this slender native shrub are usually opposite or whorled and, as in the species above, are poisonous. The flowers, ½ inch or less across, are usually a darker rose than those of the Mountain Laurel.

A southeastern variety that occurs both in rocky woodlands and bogs in our mountains and in sandy woodlands, savannahs, and bogs in the coastal plain. *April-June.* (145-8-2)

Ericaceae

ZENOBIA

Zenobia pulverulenta (Bartr.) Pollard

A shrub from 2-8 feet or more in height, with tardily deciduous leaves about 1 inch wide. The fragrant flowers have a broadly campanulate corolla ¼ inch or more long.

These handsome plants, native to the coastal plain of Virginia, North Carolina, and South Carolina, grow in bogs and in low thickets of woody evergreens known as "bays." *April-June.* *(145-9-1)*

FETTER-BUSH; MOUNTAIN ANDROMEDA

Pieris floribunda (Pursh) Bentham & Hooker

This small shrub, seldom more than 3-4 feet tall, has alternate, evergreen leaves about 2 inches long and compact terminal clusters of numerous, strongly urceolate or urn-shaped flowers.

Although widely cultivated, this *Pieris* is native only to the southern Appalachians and is found in our area only on the high mountain balds in a few western counties. *May-June.* *(145-10-1)*

Ericaceae

LYONIA; FETTER-BUSH

Lyonia lucida (Lam.) K. Koch

The young branches of this evergreen shrub are sharply 3-angled. The urn-shaped flowers, about ¼ inch long, are borne in short, axillary clusters.

Native to the coastal plain of the southeastern U.S., Lyonia grows in low woods, pocosins, and the savannahs of our eastern counties. A related species, *Lyonia ligustrina,* occurs in a variety of moist habitats essentially throughout the state. *April-May.* *(145-11-3)*

FETTER-BUSH; LEUCOTHOË

Leucothoë axillaris (Lam.) D. Don

The tough, clustered, arching stems of this evergreen native shrub are usually 2-4 feet or more long, and the compact, axillary racemes of small urceolate flowers are to 3 inches long.

Primarily found in the southeastern U.S., Leucothoë grows in "bays," in thickets, or along streams at scattered localities over most of the state except the lower piedmont. *April-May.* *(145-12-2)*

Ericaceae

LEUCOTHOË

Leucothoë recurva (Buckl.) Gray

Unlike the previous species, these low, spreading shrubs have deciduous leaves. The urceolate or urn-shaped corolla consists of 5 fused petals with only the small, recurved tips separate.

Native to the southern Appalachians, these plants grow in bogs and rocky woods in our mountains. A somewhat similar species with deciduous leaves, *L. racemosa,* grows chiefly in our coastal plain and piedmont. *April-June.* *(145-12-3)*

SOURWOOD

Oxydendrum arboreum (L.) DeCandolle

The numerous, small, urn-shaped flowers, each less than ¼ inch long, are borne in profusion in flat sprays. They produce the nectar from which the prized, water-clear Sourwood honey is derived.

Widespread over the eastern U.S., and often cultivated, these native trees are relatively frequent in open, well-drained, deciduous woodlands essentially throughout the state. *June-July.* *(145-13-1)*

Ericaceae

TRAILING ARBUTUS*

Epigaea repens Linnaeus

This prostrate, woody perennial has small, very fragrant flowers and alternate, ovate, evergreen leaves 1-2 inches long.

There are only 2 species of *Epigaea*, 1 in the southeastern U.S. and another in Japan. Our species grows in dry, sandy or rocky woodlands at scattered localities throughout the state. *February-April.* *(145-15-1)*

WINTERGREEN; CHECKERBERRY

Gaultheria procumbens Linnaeus

Also called "Teaberry," the leaves of these low, upright, evergreen perennials are very aromatic. The small, urceolate flowers, about ¼ inch long, are followed by fleshy, red, berry-like fruits.

Primarily a plant of the northeastern U.S., Wintergreen grows in varied woodland habitats, chiefly in our mountains and coastal plain, where it is near its southern limit. *June-August.* *(145-16-1)*

BLUEBERRY

Vaccinium corymbosum Linnaeus

The cultivated Blueberries of commerce were developed from these variable native shrubs. Plants of this species of *Vaccinium* are usually more than 3 feet tall and, like the other Blueberries, have small, urn-shaped flowers.

Native to much of the eastern U.S., Blueberries grow in pine or deciduous woodlands and along woodland borders in the mountains and in low areas of our coastal plain. *March-May.* *(145-19-8)*

BEARBERRY

Vaccinium erythrocarpum Michaux

An upright shrub that can be identified easily by the quite distinctive slender, red, 4-parted flowers. The deciduous leaves are finely serrate, lanceolate, and 2-3 inches long.

A native of the southern Appalachians, these plants are occasionally found in the high mountains of western North Carolina where they grow in moist woodlands and bogs. *May-July.* *(145-19-13)*

Ericaceae

CRANBERRY

Vaccinium macrocarpon Aiton

This is another native member of the Heath family that has been domesticated. The small flowers of these creeping, woody perennials are followed in the fall by the edible berries that may be up to ½ inch in diameter.

A northern or northeastern species that is found in North Carolina only in a few bogs of our mountains and coastal plain. *May-July.* *(145-19-14)*

Diapensiaceae

OCONEE BELLS*

Shortia galacifolia Torrey & Gray

As the specific name implies, this low, attractive perennial has glossy evergreen leaves resembling those of *Galax* which is also a member of the same small family. The bell-shaped, 5-petaled flowers are about ¾ inch long.

A rare plant that grows along stream banks in rich woods in a very few counties in the mountains of North and South Carolina and Georgia. *March-April.* *(146-1-1)*

Diapensiaceae

PIXIE MOSS*

Pyxidanthera barbulata Michaux

A prostrate, creeping, woody perennial with evergreen, lanceolate leaves about ¼ inch long and small, sessile flowers about ¼ inch across.

Pixie Moss is rare and irregularly distributed in the dry sandy woods and pine barrens of the coastal plain from northern South Carolina to New Jersey. Our specimens are found chiefly south of the Neuse River. *March-April.* (146-2-1)

GALAX

Galax aphylla Linnaeus

The leathery, 3-4 inch wide leaves of these low, rhizomatous perennials turn reddish brown or bronze in the winter and are often used in Christmas decorations. The flower stalk is usually 18-24 inches tall.

Native to the southern Appalachian region but cultivated elsewhere, Galax grows in open, often rocky, deciduous woods in our mountains and, less frequently, in the piedmont and coastal plain. *May-July.* (146-3-1)

SHOOTING STAR*

Dodecatheon meadia Linnaeus

An often cultivated herbaceous perennial with wide, smooth leaves and a flowering stalk 12-18 inches tall. The flowers may be lilac, pale pink, or white.

Primarily a woodland plant found on neutral or basic soils, Shooting Star is more frequent in the north-central U.S. In our area it occurs at a few scattered localities in the mountains and piedmont. *April-May.* (147-1-1)

FRINGED LOOSESTRIFE

Lysimachia ciliata Linnaeus

The opposite, ovate to lanceolate leaves of this plant have fringed petioles. A usually solitary, slender-stalked flower, about 1 inch across, is in the axil of each of the upper leaves.

These rhizomatous perennials, often 3 feet or more tall, are native to the eastern U.S. With us they grow in alluvial woods or on moist slopes in many widely separated places chiefly in our mountains and piedmont.
June-August. (147-2-1)

Primulaceae

WHORLED LOOSESTRIFE

Lysimachia quadrifolia Linnaeus

The leaves of these 12-18 inch tall, unbranched perennials are in whorls of 4 to 6. A single flower, about ½ inch across, is borne on a very slender stalk arising from the axil of each of the upper leaves.

A species of the northeastern U.S. irregularly distributed throughout North Carolina, these plants usually grow in full sun in clearings or along woodland margins. *May-July.* *(147-2-6)*

Symplocaceae

HORSE-SUGAR; SWEETLEAF

Symplocos tinctoria (L.) L'Heritier

A deciduous shrub or small tree, sometimes cultivated, that usually flowers before the leaves appear. The compact clusters of small, fragrant, cream-colored flowers, borne in profusion along the branches of the previous year's growth, are quite conspicuous in the early spring woods.

Primarily of southeastern distribution, Horse-sugar grows in sandy thickets, in alluvial woods, and along streams in all parts of North Carolina except the upper piedmont. *March-May.* *(151-1-1)*

Styracaceae

STORAX

Styrax americana Lamarck

An attractive, bushy shrub 5-10 feet tall with glossy, deciduous leaves 1-3 inches long and nodding, 5-petaled flowers about ½ inch long.

Native to the southeastern U.S., Storax grows in swamp forests, in low woods, and along stream banks of our coastal plain. *April-June.* *(152-2-2)*

Oleaceae

FRINGE TREE; OLD MAN'S BEARD*

Chionanthus virginicus Linnaeus

A deciduous, often cultivated shrub or small tree with smooth, opposite, ovate to elliptic leaves usually 3-6 inches long and large, drooping clusters of small, fragrant flowers, the narrow, linear petals of which are about 1 inch long.

Primarily limited to the coastal states of the southeastern U.S., Fringe Trees grow in dry woods more or less throughout our state.
April-May. *(153-3-1)*

Loganiaceae

YELLOW JESSAMINE

Gelsemium sempervirens (L.) Aiton

These trailing or climbing woody vines have slender, wiry stems and evergreen, lanceolate leaves. The fragrant flowers, an inch or more long, often occur in sufficient numbers to make the plant quite showy. This is the state flower of South Carolina.

Indigenous to the southeastern U.S., this vine is common in thickets, in open woodlands, and along roadsides throughout our coastal plain. *March-April.* *(154-1-1)*

Gentianaceae

SABATIA; ROSE-PINK

Sabatia angularis (L.) Pursh

The 1-3 foot stem of this native biennial is strongly 4-angled as indicated by the specific name. The showy, fragrant flowers are about 1 inch across.

Plants of this native species are widespread over much of the eastern U.S. In North Carolina they are infrequent but may be found occasionally along woodland borders and marshes at scattered localities primarily in our piedmont and lower mountains. *July-August.* *(155-1-5)*

SEA PINK; MARSH PINK

Sabatia stellaris Pursh

Although closely related to the preceeding species, these plants grow in a different habitat, are usually less than 2 feet tall, have narrower and more elongate leaves, and flowers up to 1½ inches across.

As the common name implies, the Sea Pink occurs in moist depressions and brackish marshes of the outer coastal plain, ranging from New England to Florida and Louisiana.

July-October. (155-1-6)

FRINGED GENTIAN*

Gentiana crinita Froelich

A native annual or biennial, often 1-2 feet tall, which bears attractive flowers about 1½ inches long with 4 fringed petals.

These rare plants are known from damp meadows and seepage slopes in only 2 of our mountain counties, where they are near the southern limit of their range. *September-October.* (155-2-1)

AGUE-WEED; STIFF GENTIAN*

Gentiana quinquefolia Linnaeus

The rather narrow, erect, 5-lobed flowers of this annual herb are about ¾ inch long; the angled stems and branches are slightly winged.

A species of the eastern U.S., restricted in North Carolina to the mountains where it grows on moist roadbanks and the margins of streams or bogs. *September-October.* (155-2-2)

SAMPSON'S SNAKEROOT*

Gentiana villosa Linnaeus

These native perennials, 8-24 inches tall, are glabrous or smooth and not villous or hairy as the specific name mistakenly implies. The wide leaves are usually about 2-3 inches long.

Primarily southeastern in distribution, this rare Gentian is found at scattered localities in open woods and pinelands in all 3 provinces of the state. *September-November.* (155-2-4)

SOAPWORT GENTIAN*

Gentiana saponaria Linnaeus

These perennials, with large terminal flowers up to 2 inches long, do not produce a lather but derive their common name from the resemblance of their foliage to that of *Saponaria* or Soapwort.

A rare plant, native to the eastern U.S., that occurs in bogs, marshes, and low ditches at widely scattered localities in a few counties in each of our 3 provinces.

September-November. (155-2-8)

PENNYWORT

Obolaria virginica Linnaeus

The thick, rounded, opposite, purplish green leaves of this low, native perennial are only ½ inch or less long. The small white to lavender flowers are solitary or in clusters of 3 in the axils of the upper leaves.

Essentially a species of the rich, deciduous forests of the southeastern U.S., Pennywort is found chiefly in the mountains and the northern piedmont of North Carolina. Because of its inconspicuous coloration, it is often overlooked. *March-May.* (155-5-1)

BLUE STAR*

Amsonia tabernaemontana Walter

This slender, leafy, perennial herb, with 1 to several 1-3 foot stems from a single root-crown, has leaves that are quite variable in width. The flowers are about ½ inch across.

Native to the eastern and central U.S., in our area this *Amsonia* grows on wooded slopes and in bottomlands, primarily in the piedmont counties. *April.* (156-1-1)

INDIAN HEMP

Apocynum cannabinum Linnaeus

An often rank, perennial herb 1-3 feet tall with milky sap and tough, fibrous stems from which it gets its common name. The open clusters of minute flowers do not extend beyond the leaves, which are ovate or elliptic and 1-3 inches long.

Widespread over the eastern U.S., Indian Hemp is frequently found throughout our state along roadsides, along dry woodland margins, and in recent clearings.
May-July. (156-3-1)

Apocynaceae

SPREADING DOGBANE

Apocynum androsaemifolium Linnaeus

The larger, fragrant, almost showy flowers of these plants are ¼ inch or more long and distinguish it immediately from the previous species. The fruits of both are slender follicles 3-6 inches long but only about ⅛ inch in diameter.

These perennials, more northern in their general distribution, grow along roadsides and woodland margins only in our mountains. *June-August.* *(156-3-3)*

Asclepiadaceae

SWAMP MILKWEED

Asclepias incarnata ssp. *pulchra* (Ehrh. ex Willd.) Woodson

These native perennials with milky sap may have 1 or several 2-5 foot stalks from a single rootstock. The flowers are arranged in globose clusters usually 1-2 inches in diameter.

More frequent northward, it is a conspicuous but not common plant of marshes and moist meadows in our mountains, piedmont, and northern coastal plain. *July-September.* *(157-1-1)*

BUTTERFLY WEED; PLEURISY-ROOT

Asclepias tuberosa Linnaeus

Unlike our other species of *Asclepias,* this perennial has clear sap and alternate leaves 2-3 inches long. Often cultivated for its brilliant flowers, it may have several 1-2 foot stems from a single root-crown.

Native over much of the eastern U.S., it is relatively frequent in dry fields, on roadsides, and along woodland margins throughout our area.

May-August. (157-1-4)

ASCLEPIAS

Asclepias lanceolata Walter

This slender, native perennial, 3-5 feet tall, with narrow, opposite, lanceolate leaves 6-8 inches long, produces only a few small clusters of brilliant reddish orange flowers.

Occurring on the Atlantic coastal plain from Florida to New Jersey, it is rare to infrequent in North Carolina where it grows on savannahs and in moist ditches and brackish marshes. *June-August.* (157-1-6)

MILKWEED

Asclepias syriaca Linnaeus

A coarse, rhizomatous perennial, often 4-6 feet tall, with numerous fragrant flowers in large, umbellate clusters 2-3 inches in diameter. The young shoots are said to be edible when boiled.

These plants are native to the north and central U.S. and appear in our area in the northern mountains and piedmont where they grow, often in large colonies, in meadows and along fencerows, roadsides, and forest margins. *June-August.* *(157-1-10)*

VARIEGATED MILKWEED

Asclepias variegata Linnaeus

An attractive perennial herb 2-3 feet tall which has 2-4 compact, umbellate flower clusters 1-2 inches in diameter.

Not common but found at scattered localities essentially throughout the state, this Milkweed grows in open deciduous woodlands and along forest margins; it is native to the eastern U.S. *May-June.* *(157-1-12)*

Asclepiadaceae

CLIMBING MILKWEED

Matelea carolinensis (Jacq.) Woodson

These twining herbaceous vines with milky sap have heart-shaped leaves that are usually 2-4 inches long. The maroon flowers, about ¾ inch across, are pollinated by flies.

Native to the southeastern U.S., these perennials are infrequent in the open, deciduous woods and along stream banks in the piedmont of North Carolina. *April-June.* (157-3-5)

Convolvulaceae

DODDER; LOVE VINE

Cuscuta rostrata Engelmann

There are in North Carolina 8 species of this slender, orange-stemmed, parasitic genus of the Morning Glory family. Some are parasitic on clover and other herbaceous plants, and some are parasitic on woody plants. The flowers of all our species are small, usually less than ⅛ inch across.

This species, native to the southern Appalachians, is found on woody and semi-woody plants (often Blackberry) in our mountains. *August-September.* (158-1-7)

Convolvulaceae

MORNING GLORY

Ipomoea purpurea (L.) Roth

These herbaceous, annual, twining vines, introduced into the U.S. as garden plants, have become thoroughly naturalized. The showy flowers, lasting only a few hours, are about 2 inches in diameter.

A common weed in cultivated and fallow fields, along roadsides, and in waste places throughout the state. *July-September.* *(158-7-4)*

MORNING GLORY

Ipomoea sagittata Cavanilles

This native perennial Morning Glory, with rose-lavender flowers 2-3 inches broad, is easily distinguished from the preceeding one by the narrow, spear-shaped leaves and a distinctive habitat.

This southeastern species grows on moist, sandy roadsides and along the margins of brackish marshes of the outer coastal plain of North Carolina, which is its northern limit. *July-September.* *(158-7-9)*

Convolvulaceae

MORNING GLORY

Ipomoea macrorhiza Michaux

A robust perennial vine with pubescent, crinkled leaves (the lower ones often 3-lobed), a pubescent calyx, and large flowers 3 inches in diameter. Note that the species below has smooth leaves and a glabrous caylx.

A rare plant in our state known only from sandy clearings and beaches around Southport, where it was probably introduced from further south. *June-July.* *(158-7-10)*

MAN-ROOT; MORNING GLORY

Ipomoea pandurata (L.) G. F. W. Meyer

Often several to many, long, trailing, usually purple stems grow from the crown of the large starchy root of this herbaceous perennial which has flowers somewhat similar to the above species, but which has smooth leaves and glabrous calyces.

This widespread and relatively common native of the eastern U.S. is found throughout North Carolina on open, often dry roadsides, in old fields, and along fencerows. *June-September.* *(158-7-11)*

Polemoniaceae

MOSS PINK

Phlox subulata Linnaeus

A prostrate, semi-evergreen perennial with small, awl-shaped leaves and ½-¾ inch broad flowers with petals that are either entire or notched at the end.

Often cultivated, Moss Pink is native to the northeastern U.S. and grows in only a few of our mountain counties on dry, open, rocky slopes. A similar species, *P. nivalis*, is found in the piedmont and part of the coastal plain. *April.* *(159-1-3)*

PHLOX

Phlox amoena Sims

This low perennial *Phlox,* 6-12 inches tall, bears flowers, about ¾ inch across, in compact clusters at the ends of pubescent stems.

This southeastern species occurs occasionally in dry woodlands and on open banks in a few of our mountain and upper piedmont counties, where it is near the northern limit of its range.
April-June. *(159-1-5)*

Polemoniaceae

PHLOX

Phlox carolina Linnaeus

The 1 to several flowering stems of this showy perennial may be 3 feet or more tall. The compact terminal inflorescence, with individual flowers ½-¾ inch across, is usually about as broad as long.

This southeastern species, often cultivated, is found in deciduous woods and along forest margins more or less throughout our state. It intergrades with 2 other tall species of Phlox that have a more northern range. *May-July.* (159-1-9)

Hydrophyllaceae

WATER LEAF

Hydrophyllum virginianum Linnaeus

This herbaceous perennial, 1-2 feet tall, has pinnately divided leaves and small, rather inconspicuous flowers with the stamens exserted well beyond the ¼ inch long corolla.

Native to the northeastern U.S., Water Leaf grows in rich woods and along stream banks in our mountains and less frequently in the piedmont. *April-June.* (160-4-3)

Hydrophyllaceae

PHACELIA

Phacelia bipinnatifida Michaux

This native, glandular-pubescent biennial, usually 1-2 feet tall, bears bell-shaped flowers about ½ inch broad. As the specific name implies, the 2-3 inch long leaves are twice pinnately divided.

More common westward in the central U.S., these plants are infrequent in our mountain counties where they grow on rocky slopes, along creek banks, and in deciduous woods. *April-May.* *(160-5-1)*

SCORPION WEED

Phacelia purshii Buckley

These small annuals, usually 6-12 inches tall, but occasionally with stems reaching a length of 20 inches, have pubescent, pinnately cleft or parted leaves to 1½ inches long. Each inflorescence usually has 10-30 flowers with lightly fringed corollas about ¼ inch broad.

Rare in our area, these plants range primarily west of the Appalachians; they grow in moist meadows and on moist roadsides in only 2 of our mountain counties. *May-June.* *(160-5-5)*

Hydrophyllaceae

FRINGED PHACELIA

Phacelia fimbriata Michaux

Also annuals, these plants are closely related to the preceeding species of *Phacelia* but differ in several respects: there are fewer flowers in the inflorescence of the Fringed Phacelia and, as the name implies, the petals are more deeply fringed.

Native to the southern Appalachians this *Phacelia* is known from only 4 of our mountain counties where it grows, sometimes in showy masses, along stream banks and in low woodlands.

April-May. (160-5-6)

Boraginaceae

BLUE WEED; VIPER'S BUGLOSS

Echium vulgare Linnaeus

A bristly, often weedy, introduced biennial usually 1-2 feet or more tall. The numerous buds are in a tight coil that slowly straightens as new flowers open from the base to the tip of the inflorescence; the zygomorphic flowers, ¼-½ inch long, turn pink with age.

These plants are found in dry pastures and along roadsides in a few of our mountain and piedmont counties.

June-September. (161-4-1)

Verbenaceae

BEAUTY BERRY

Callicarpa americana Linnaeus

The axillary clusters of small flowers of this shrub are seldom noticed. However, the compact fruit clusters, an inch or more in diameter, are quite showy in late summer and give the bush its common name.

Primarily a species of the southeastern U.S., Beauty Berry grows in moist, usually sandy woodlands and clearings at scattered localities chiefly on our coastal plain. *June-July.* (162-4-1)

Lamiaceae

WOOD SAGE

Teucrium canadense Linnaeus

The stiff erect stems of this stoloniferous perennial may be from 1-3 feet tall, and the serrate, lanceolate, 1-2 inch wide leaves may be nearly glabrous (as in the plant shown) or heavily pubescent.

Native to the eastern U.S., Wood Sage is found growing in low woodlands, moist meadows, and marshes at scattered localities in all provinces of North Carolina.
June-August. (164-3-1)

OBEDIENT PLANT; PHYSOSTEGIA

Dracocephalum virginianum Linnaeus

Glabrous, stoloniferous perennials, 1-3 feet tall, with 4 rows of 1 inch long zygomorphic flowers. The common name comes from the tendency of a flower, once pushed to one side, to remain in the new position.

Often cultivated, *Physostegia* is native to the northeastern U.S. In our area it grows in bogs and low meadows of the mountains and, much less frequently and more scattered, in the piedmont and coastal plain. *August-September.* (164-13-1)

HENBIT

Lamium amplexicaule Linnaeus

The square stems, opposite leaves, and, on close inspection, the attractive 2-lipped flowers identify this as a member of the Mint family.

An introduced annual, Henbit is a common weed in lawns, pastures, cultivated fields, and on roadsides throughout the state and much of the eastern U.S. *March-May.* (164-19-1)

HEDGE NETTLE

Stachys latidens Small

As with other members of this family, the flowers of this perennial mint are bilaterally symmetrical or zygomorphic. The coarsely toothed leaves are 4-6 inches long.

Five species of *Stachys* occur in North Carolina. This one, a native of the southern Appalachians, grows in marshes, wet meadows, and woodlands of the mountains. *June-August.* (164-20-5)

LYRE-LEAVED SAGE

Salvia lyrata Linnaeus

The pinnately lobed to divided lyrate leaves of this herbaceous perennial are mostly basal and form a winter rosette from which grows the 12-18 inch flowering stalk.

A weedy native of the eastern U.S., this *Salvia* grows on roadsides and in lawns and meadows throughout the state.
April-May. (164-22-1)

SKULLCAP

Scutellaria integrifolia Linnaeus

These perennial herbs, unlike most other members of the Mint family, are not aromatic. The pubescent 1-2 foot stems bear strongly 2-lipped flowers, about 1 inch long.

Native to the eastern U.S., Skullcap is found throughout our state growing in pine woods, in low meadows, and on roadsides and savannahs.
May-July. (164-5-5)

BEE-BALM; OSWEGO TEA

Monarda didyma Linnaeus

The compact, crown-like whorl of showy flowers, with brightly colored, leaf-like bracts just below it, is 3-4 inches in diameter.

These strong-scented perennials, 3-6 feet tall, native to the northeastern U.S., are widely planted as ornamentals. In our area they are infrequent on spring banks in the mountains. *July-September.* (164-23-1)

DOTTED HORSEMINT

Monarda punctata Linnaeus

Visible just below the compact whorl of lightly purple-spotted yellow flowers, a series of lavender or white bracts makes even more colorful the 1-2 inch broad inflorescence of this perennial.

Primarily a species of the Atlantic and Gulf coastal plains, Dotted Horsemint is relatively common in the coastal plain and frequent to infrequent in the piedmont. It grows in sandy or rocky fields and open woods. *August-September.* (164-23-4)

MOUNTAIN MINT

Pycnanthemum muticum (Michx.) Persoon

This strong-scented, rhizomatous perennial, usually with several erect stems 1-4 feet tall from a single root-crown, has lanceolate leaves 1-3 inches long. The small flowers are in compact heads about ½ inch broad.

Plants of the eastern and central U.S., they grow, despite the name, in savannahs, bogs, and low woods at scattered localities chiefly in our mountains and coastal plain. *July-August.* (164-28-4)

HORSE NETTLE

Solanum carolinense Linnaeus

This prickly, rhizomatous perennial has simple or weakly branched stems usually 8-24 inches tall and flowers about 1 inch broad. The naked, globular, dull berries that follow are about ½ inch in diameter.

A weedy native of the eastern U.S. that grows in old fields, gardens, waste places, and on roadsides throughout the state.
May-July. (165-5-5)

APPLE OF PERU

Nicandra physalodes (L.) Persoon

A glabrous annual, 1-3 feet tall, with succlent stems and a 1½ inch broad corolla of 5 fused petals. The fleshy berry is hidden by the 5-angled, inflated calyx that looks like a minature Japanese lantern.

Introduced from South America, these weedy plants are now naturalized in our area in fields and waste places at scattered localities, chiefly in the mountains. *July-September.* (165-2-1)

HEDGE HYSSOP

Gratiola viscidula Pennell

These slender, somewhat fleshy stemmed, unbranched perennials are usually 6-18 inches tall. The small, light lavender flowers, solitary in each leaf axil, are a little more than ¼ inch long.

A northern species found in bogs, marshes, and wet ditches at scattered localities in all 3 provinces of North Carolina. *June-September.* (166-7-4)

MONKEY FLOWER

Mimulus ringens Linnaeus

The square stem of this glabrous perennial is 2-5 feet tall, but unlike the closely related *Mimulus alatus,* the angles are not winged. The strongly 2-lipped flowers of both species are 1 inch or more long.

In our area Monkey Flower occurs chiefly in the mountains and upper piedmont where it grows in marshes, bogs, wet meadows, and along stream banks; its primary range is the north-eastern U.S.

June-September. (166-11-2)

WOOLLY MULLEIN; MOTH MULLEIN

Verbascum thapsus Linnaeus

These rank, woolly-pubescent, yellowish green biennials produce flower stalks 1-5 feet or more tall. The fragrant flowers, about ¾ inch broad, are in clusters of 3 in a compact elongate inflorescence; the center flower of each cluster opens first.

An introduced European weed, common along roadsides, in fallow fields, pastures, and waste places essentially throughout the state.

June-September. (166-12-3)

TURTLEHEAD

Chelone cuthbertii Small

The very strongly 4-ranked flowers and the sessile leaves of this species are distinctive. The zygomorphic flowers, about 1½ inches long, are at the end of slender stems 2-3 feet long.

These rather rare perennials, native to the southeastern U.S., grow along stream banks and in wet meadows or bogs in a few of our mountain counties. *July-September.* (166-13-1)

Scrophulariaceae

TURTLEHEAD; CHELONE

Chelone glabra Linnaeus

The leaves of this variable species have short petioles and the flowers, though the same size as those of the preceding species, are not arranged in 4 strict ranks.

This perennial, native primarily to the northeastern U.S., grows in low, moist meadows and thickets at widely scattered localities in all 3 provinces of the state but is nowhere common. *August-October.* (166-13-4)

BEARD TONGUE; PENSTEMON

Penstemon canescens Britton

An erect, pubescent, often sticky perennial with flower stalks 1-2 feet tall. The 2-lipped flowers are about 1 inch long and have one sterile bearded stamen, thus the common name.

Native to the general area of the Appalachians, these plants grow on rocky banks and roadsides and in meadows, in the mountains and a few counties in the upper piedmont. *May-July.* (166-14-2)

TOAD FLAX

Linaria canadensis (L.) Dumont

The erect 1-2 foot flowering stems of this annual or biennial arise from a basal rosette of short, prostrate, sterile stems. The strongly 2-lipped flowers are usually about ¼ inch long; however, plants with flowers up to ½ inch long, such as shown here, sometimes occur in some areas.

A weed in fallow fields, frequently growing in colorful masses with *Rumex,* this native to the eastern U.S., is found throughout our coastal plain and piedmont. *March-May.* *(166-16-1)*

VERONICA; SPEEDWELL

Veronica persica Poiret

The flowers of this low, introduced annual are ¼-½ inch broad and, unlike the flowers of most other members of this family, they appear to have only 4 petals, 2 of the usual 5 petals being completely fused.

A colorful weed in lawns and along roadsides at numerous scattered localities in our mountains and piedmont. *March-June.* *(166-20-5)*

Scrophulariaceae

FALSE FOXGLOVE

Aureolaria pedicularia (L.) Rafinesque

These spreading, branched, glandular-pubescent annuals, 1-3 feet tall, with flowers over 1 inch long, are semi-parasitic on the roots of trees in the Black Oak group.

A native of the eastern U.S., this *Aureolaria* grows in sandy woodlands and open, dry, deciduous forests locally throughout the state. *September-October.* (166-24-1)

DOWNY FALSE FOXGLOVE

Aureolaria virginica (L.) Pennell

The erect unbranched flowering stems of this species may be 3-4 feet tall and the flowers 1½ inches long.

Native to the eastern U.S., these perennials are semi-parasitic on the roots of trees of the White Oak group. They grow in or along the margins of deciduous woodlands over most of the state. *May-July.* (166-24-3)

GERARDIA

Agalinis purpurea (L.) Pennell

These annuals, semi-parasitic on the roots of grasses, are often profusely branched and may be 2-3 feet tall. The flowers are about 1 inch long and nearly as broad.

A colorful, sporadic weed along low roadsides, it is native to the pond margins, roadsides and low meadows of the eastern U.S., and occurs locally in all provinces of North Carolina.

September-October. *(166-25-3)*

INDIAN PAINT BRUSH

Castilleja coccinea (L.) Sprengel

The bracts, or modified leaves, beneath the flowers of this pubescent annual or biennial herb are cleft into 3-5 segments and are more brilliantly colored than the slender, inch long flowers.

More common northward, plants of this species, semi-parasitic on the roots of grasses, grow in moist meadows and along woodland margins chiefly in our mountains and, less frequently, in the piedmont.

April-May. *(166-28-1)*

Scrophulariaceae

WOOD BETONY; LOUSEWORT

Pedicularis canadensis Linnaeus

Perennial, pubescent herbs, usually 6-12 inches tall, with yellow or yellow and red flowers in a compact spike 1 inch or more in diameter. The fern-like leaves of the flowering stalk are alternate.

Relatively infrequent in moist, deciduous woodlands of the mountains and piedmont of North Carolina, Wood Betony is native to the eastern U.S. A fall flowering species, *P. lanceolata,* with opposite stem leaves, occurs in our southwestern mountains. *May-July.* (166-29-1)

Bignoniaceae

TRUMPET CREEPER; COW-ITCH VINE

Campsis radicans (L.) Seemann

This native woody vine, sometimes cultivated for the showy, trumpet-shaped, 3-4 inch long flowers, often becomes a troublesome weed.

Only this species of *Campsis* occurs in the southeastern U.S.; a second is native to Asia. Trumpet Creeper grows along fence rows and the margins of low woods and thickets throughout our state, although it is infrequent in the mountains.
June-July. (167-2-1)

Bignoniaceae

CROSS VINE

Anisostichus capreolata (L.) Bureau

A woody vine, with colorful flowers 2-3 inches long, that often grows to the tops of tall trees clinging to the bark by means of tendrils at the end of each leaf and by small rootlets.

Often found growing in alluvial forests and deciduous woods, chiefly of our piedmont and coastal plain, these handsome plants are native to the southeastern U.S. *April-May.* *(167-1-1)*

INDIAN CIGAR; CATAWBA TREE

Catalpa speciosa Warder ex Engelmann

The long, slender fruits of this tree, sometimes smoked by children, account for the common name. The large flowers, up to 2 inches long, are variously marked with yellow and purple in the center.

This tree, native to the central U.S., is widely planted, and often escaped, in many of the eastern states. It grows on road banks and in waste places at a few localities in our piedmont and mountains. *May-June.* *(167-3-2)*

SQUAW ROOT; CANCER ROOT

Conopholis americana (L.) Wallroth

The numerous, thick, yellowish brown stems of this parasitic herb are 2-6 inches long and often form large clumps on the roots of oak trees. The leaves are reduced to small, brown scales.

Native chiefly to the northeastern U.S., Squaw Root occurs in dry oak forests at scattered localities, chiefly in our mountains. *April-June.* (169-2-1)

BUTTERWORT

Pinguicula pumila Michaux

Tiny insects are trapped by the sticky leaves of this low perennial, thus it is called "carnivorous," as are the 2 following members of this interesting plant family. The flowers are about ¾ inch long, including the slender spur.

A rare native of only a few southeastern states, these plants are known from only 3 of our coastal plain counties where they grow in low pinelands and savannahs. *April-May.* *(170-1-1)*

BLADDERWORT

Utricularia inflata Walter

The whorl of inflated leaves forms a floating platform from which the 4-6 inch flower stalk arises. The mass of modified, bladder-like, submersed leaves trap small larvae and fish.

These plants of the southeastern U.S. are irregularly distributed in ponds, pools, and roadside ditches at a few widely scattered localities in the coastal plain. *May-October.* *(170-2-5)*

Lentibulariaceae

BLADDERWORT

Utricularia purpurea Walter

While the flowers of this small aquatic are only ¼-½ inch long, they sometimes form colorful patches against the dark water of shallow pools and roadside ditches. This Bladderwort, native over much of the eastern U.S. but rare in our area, is known from only a few counties of the coastal plain. *May-September.* *(170-2-4)*

Rubiaceae

BUTTON BUSH

Cephalanthus occidentalis Linnaeus

The compact, globose inflorescence of this shrub is 1-2 inches in diameter and is made up of many small flowers with exserted anthers. The opposite, usually glabrous leaves are mostly 2-5 inches long.

Native to much of the northern, eastern, and southern U.S., Button Bush grows along streams, by ponds and lakes, and in low open areas over most of North Carolina.

June-August. *(173-2-1)*

Rubiaceae

PARTRIDGE BERRY

Mitchella repens Linnaeus

The small, fragrant, trumpet-shaped flowers of this prostrate, creeping perennial always occur in pairs. Later, the 2 developing ovularies fuse to form a single berry-like fruit ¼ inch or more broad. A native of the eastern U.S., *Mitchella* is found in low deciduous woods more or less throughout our state. *May-June.* (173-7-1)

BLUETS

Houstonia caerulea Linnaeus

These delicate but colorful small perennials, here shown slightly larger than natural size, grow in clumps and spread by slender rhizomes. The thin flower stalks may be from 1-3 inches or more tall.

Essentially a northeastern species, Bluets are common in lawns, clearings, and forest margins throughout the state, though infrequent in the coastal plain. *April-May.* (173-8-1)

Rubiaceae

HOUSTONIA

Houstonia purpurea Linnaeus

Much less showy than the preceeding species, these perennial herbs have 1 to several upright leafy stems, 4-16 inches high, from a single root-crown. The leaves, mostly 1½ inches long, may be glabrous or densely pubescent.

Native from Maryland to Georgia and inland to the central U.S., this *Houstonia* is found in deciduous woods primarily in our mountains and piedmont. *May-June.* (173-8-5)

Caprifoliaceae

BUSH HONEYSUCKLE

Diervilla sessilifolia Buckley

A low shrub with simple, opposite leaves that, as the specific name implies, are usually sessile, at least near the ends of the branches.

These plants, growing on bluffs and roadbanks in only a few of our mountain counties, are native to a rather restricted area of the southern Appalachians. *June-August.* (174-1-2)

Caprifoliaceae

CORAL HONEYSUCKLE

Lonicera sempervirens Linnaeus

A glabrous, twining vine, with the opposite leaves just below the inflorescence fused around the stem. The united petals form a slender trumpet-shaped flower nearly 2 inches long.

These perennials, sometimes cultivated, are native to the southeastern states and grow in clearings and along the margins of deciduous woodlands in our coastal plain and piedmont. *March-May.* (174-2-5)

HONEYSUCKLE

Lonicera japonica Thunberg

This twining, woody vine, introduced long ago from Japan as an ornamental, is often a bad weed, strangling or shading the native vegetation. The wonderfully fragrant flowers, an inch or more long, occasionally justify its existence.

Honeysuckle is common in waste places and low woodlands throughout North Carolina and much of the eastern U.S. *April-June.* (174-2-4)

LONICERA

Lonicera dioica Linnaeus

These vines have elliptic to oblong, opposite leaves, usually 3-5 inches long, that may be petiolate, sessile, or connate on flowering stems; the red zygomorphic flowers are about 1 inch long and are borne in compact clusters. The red berries are about ¼-½ inch long.

A rare perennial native to the woodlands and thickets of a few of our mountain counties; it is more common northward.

June-August. (174-2-6)

HOBBLE-BUSH; MOOSE-WOOD

Viburnum alnifolium Marshall

A native, loosely branched shrub 6 or more feet tall. The showy outer flowers of the inflorescence are nearly 1 inch across and are sterile, the smaller flowers in the center are fertile.

This is a northern species that reaches our area only in the higher mountains where it grows in rich coves and along stream banks. The brilliant red fruits ripen in August. *April-June.* (174-5-1)

Caprifoliaceae

WITHEROD; HAW

Viburnum cassinoides Linnaeus

The opposite, deciduous, lanceolate leaves of Witherod are mostly 2-5 inches long; the small, ill-scented flowers are arranged in a flat inflorescence often 2-4 inches across; the fleshy fruits are blue-black.

A more northern species growing in bogs and deciduous woods of our mountains and piedmont. *May-June.* (174-5-2)

MAPLE-LEAVED VIBURNUM; ARROW-WOOD

Viburnum acerifolium Linnaeus

The opposite, deciduous leaves of this shrub are 2-5 inches wide and their similarity to maple leaves accounts for both the common and scientific names of this species of *Viburnum*. The flat inflorescence, and later the cluster of black fruits, is 2-4 inches broad.

Native to the northeastern U.S., these 3-6 foot tall shrubs grow in deciduous forests of the mountains and piedmont. *April-June.* (174-5-9)

Caprifoliaceae

ELDERBERRY

Sambucus canadensis Linnaeus

The soft, pithy, branching stems of this native shrub grow 3-10 feet tall. The flat inflorescence of small, fragrant, white flowers is often 6 inches or more broad.

These shrubs grow in moist rich soil in open pastures, in alluvial woods, and along fencerows and forest margins throughout North Carolina and much of the northeastern U.S. The fruit ripens in July or August.

May-July. (174-6-1)

RED-BERRIED ELDER

Sambucus pubens Michaux

The brown rather than white pith, the conical inflorescence of inodorous flowers, and the bright red berries separate this species from the more widespread one above.

A northern species that is found in our area only in the higher mountains where it grows in, or along the margins of, deciduous or spruce-fir forests.

May-June. (174-6-2)

VENUS' LOOKING-GLASS

Specularia perfoliata (L.) A. DeCandolle

The flowering stems of these annual herbs are 6-18 inches tall and are more or less encircled by the widely heart-shaped leaves. The open-pollinated flowers are ¼-½ inch broad; smaller flowers are cleistogamous and self-pollinated.

These common, somewhat weedy natives of the eastern U.S. grow in plowed fields, in waste places, and along roadsides throughout our area.
April-June. (178-1-1)

BELLFLOWER

Campanula americana Linnaeus

The rotate flowers of this tall, native annual are about ¾ inch broad with the long style curved abruptly upward near its tip.

These weakly branched herbs, native to the northern U.S., grow to 6 feet tall on moist banks and along woodland margins in our mountains where they are relatively frequent; they are much less frequent in the piedmont.
July-September. (178-2-1)

CARDINAL FLOWER*

Lobelia cardinalis Linnaeus

There are few more brilliant and intensely colored flowers than those of this herbaceous perennial. The flowers, 1½ inches or more long, are strongly 2-lipped, or bilaterally symmetrical, even though other members of this family, as shown on the opposite page, have radial flowers.

Cardinal Flowers are 2-4 feet tall and grow in moist, open meadows and along stream banks in scattered localities throughout this state and much of the eastern U.S. *July-October.* (178-5-1)

LOBELIA

Lobelia puberula Michaux

Three partly fused petals form the wide lower lip and 2 very narrow petals the upper lip of these zygomorphic flowers that are about ¾ inch long.

These pubescent native herbs, 1-3 feet tall, growing in varied habitats from bogs to fairly dry woodlands, range more or less throughout the state and the eastern U.S.
August-October. (178-5-6)

Campanulaceae

GREAT LOBELIA

Lobelia siphilitica Linnaeus

The unbranched stems of this course perennial grow to 3 feet or more tall and are terminated by an open raceme of 2-lipped flowers, each an inch or more long. Some species of Lobelia contain poisonous alkaloids that have been used medicinally in the past.

Native to the northern and central U.S., these plants are found only in the western mountains of North Carolina where they grow in wet meadows, in low woods, and along stream banks.

August-October. (178-5-2)

Asteraceae

CHICORY

Cichorium intybus Linnaeus

The "flowers" of this introduced weed, about 1 inch across and borne at the end of a short spur branch, are quite conspicuous during the short time they remain open. The dried roots are sometimes used to flavor coffee.

Though often seen on dry roadsides and in fields and waste places of the mountains and piedmont, Chicory is absent from much of the coastal plain.

June-October. (179-4-1)

SOW THISTLE

Sonchus asper (L.) Hill

The stem leaves and the larger basal rosette leaves of this introduced, glabrous annual have soft, spiny teeth. The stems are somewhat fleshy, usually hollow (at least near the base), and 1-3 feet tall. Note the swollen base of the flower head or inflorescence.

A weed in lawns, in waste places, and along roadsides more or less throughout North Carolina and much of the U.S.

April-July. (179-8-2)

HAWKWEED

Hieracium pratense Tausch

The leafless flowering stem of this rhizomatous perennial is 6-30 inches tall and bears several heads or inflorescences in a compact cluster. The basal leaves, 2-8 inches long, have bristly hairs on each surface.

An introduced weed, more common northward, that grows in pastures, clearings, and along roadsides in our mountains and piedmont.

May-July. (179-10-3)

GOAT'S BEARD

Tragopogon dubius Scopoli

These robust herbs, often 3 feet or more tall, have flower heads about 1 inch across followed by tawny, dandelion-like fruits in a globose cluster 2-3 inches in diameter.

Two species of these introduced biennials occur very occasionally in our area in fields, in pastures, and along roadsides. This one is known from only 4 counties and the similar, but purple-flowered, *T. porrifolius* is known from only 3 counties. *May-July.* *(179-14-1)*

DWARF DANDELION; GOAT DANDELION

Krigia montana (Michx.) Nuttall

The leafless flowering stems of these perennial herbs are 4-16 inches tall, and each bears a solitary inflorescence, or flowering head, about ½ inch broad.

These plants are native to a restricted portion of the southern Appalachians in North Carolina, Tennessee, Georgia, and South Carolina, where they grow on open rocky slopes or in crevices of cliffs. *May-September.* *(179-15-2)*

DANDELION

Taraxacum officinale Wiggers

This naturalized and now weedy perennial, once used medicinally, may have been introduced into this country as an ornamental because of its bright yellow flower heads. The young leaves are sometimes used either as a salad or a cooked vegetable. The globose cluster of fruits is 1-2 inches in diameter.

Common in lawns, pastures, and waste places and along roadsides throughout North Carolina and much of the U.S. *February-June.* (179-17-2)

CHAPTALIA

Chaptalia tomentosa Ventenant

The leaves and stems of these 6-12 inch tall perennials are quite hairy, or tomentose, as indicated by the specific name. The white flowers, in heads about 1 inch broad, turn pink with age.

A native of the southeastern U.S., Chaptalia grows on savannahs and in sandy pine barrens of our coastal plain where it reaches its northern limit. *March-May.* (179-22-1)

SWAMP THISTLE

Carduus muticus (Michx.) Persoon

The flower heads of this weakly spiny biennial are about 1½ inches in diameter.

Native to the northeastern U.S., this relatively rare species of Thistle grows in bogs, meadows, and low woodland margins at scattered localities chiefly in our mountains and piedmont.

August-October. (179-25-11)

IRONWEED

Vernonia noveboracensis (L.) Michaux

These somewhat rank perennial herbs may grow to 6 feet or more in height and produce many flower heads in a loose terminal cluster.

An inhabitant of stream margins, meadows, and low woodlands throughout most of the state except the outer coastal plain, Ironweed is native generally to the southeastern U.S.

July-September. (179-27-6)

BLAZING STAR; LIATRIS

Liatris spicata (L.) Willdenow

The stiff, erect stems of this perennial are 1-5 feet tall and bear many flower heads, each ½-¾ inch broad, in a dense spike.

Often cultivated, Liatris is native to the southeastern U.S. and grows in bogs and open woodlands here and there throughout the state. *August-September.* (179-30-1)

LIATRIS

Liatris squarrosa (L.) Michaux

This more robust and branched species of *Liatris* has flower heads an inch or more broad with spreading or squarrose bracts.

A perennial native to the southeastern U.S. that grows in North Carolina in upland woods, usually on basic soils, throughout the piedmont. It is rare in our mountains and coastal plain.

August-September. (179-30-14)

TRILISA

Trilisa paniculata (J. F. Gmel.) Cassini

These perennial herbs have flowering stems 1-5 feet tall rising from a rosette of basal leaves that are mostly 2-6 inches long. Our other species, *T. odoratissima,* has the scent of vanilla.

Native to the southeastern U.S., these plants grow in low pinelands of our coastal plain where they reach their northern limit.

September-October. (179-31-2)

JOE-PYE-WEED

Eupatorium fistulosum Barratt

These hollow-stemmed perennials, 3-7 feet tall, have whorled leaves and a large, rounded inflorescence up to a foot or more broad, made up of many small flower heads.

Indigenous to the eastern U.S., this *Eupatorium* grows in bogs, marshes, and meadows chiefly of our mountains and piedmont.

July-October. (179-34-3)

WHITE SNAKEROOT

Eupatorium rugosum Houttuyn

This variable, rhizomatous perennial may have 1 or several stems 1-4 feet tall with opposite, ovate leaves mostly 3-6 inches long. The plant is poisonous and milk from cows that have eaten it will cause "milk sickness" in humans.

These plants grow in rich woods and along woodland margins chiefly in our mountains and piedmont; they are native to the northeastern U.S. *July-October.* (179-34-21)

AGERATUM; MISTFLOWER

Eupatorium coelestinum Linnaeus

This rhizomatous perennial, with branched stems 1-3 feet tall, bears rather decorative, compact, terminal clusters of numerous bell-shaped flower heads.

Native of the southeastern U.S., Ageratum grows in damp thickets and the margins of low woods of our coastal plain and, less frequently, the piedmont. *August-October.* (179-34-24)

PUSSY-TOES; EVERLASTING

Antennaria solitaria Rydberg

Identified by the solitary flower head, these low, stoloniferous perennials are dioecious, producing only female flowers on one plant and only male flowers on another. The tomentose leaves are mostly 1-3 inches long.

A native to the general region of the Appalachians which grows in deciduous woodlands of our mountains and piedmont and, less frequently, the coastal plain. *April-May.* (179-39-1)

RABBIT TOBACCO

Gnaphalium obtusifolium Linnaeus

The flower heads, upper branches, and the under surface of the narrow 1-2 inch long leaves are white or grayish white and are sometimes used in dried flower arrangements. The strong-scented leaves, sometimes smoked by boys, account for the common name.

These variable native biennials, 1-4 feet tall, grow in old fields, pastures, and waste places throughout North Carolina and the eastern U.S. *August-October.* (179-40-1)

SEA-MYRTLE

Baccharis halimifolia Linnaeus

This shrub, 3-8 feet tall, is one of our few woody members of the Aster family. The female plant shown here is in fruit. The small, white or gray flower clusters are not conspicuous, being rather similar in general appearance to those of *Gnaphalium,* shown above.

A somewhat weedy native of the southeastern U.S. that grows in old fields, clearings, roadsides, and waste places throughout our coastal plain and much of the piedmont. *September-October.* (179-43-3)

ROBINS-PLANTAIN

Erigeron pulchellus Michaux

The flower heads of these stoloniferous perennials are an inch or more across; the villous or hairy stem, 6-12 inches long, elongates further after flowering.

This *Erigeron* is native to the eastern U.S. and grows in rich woods chiefly in our mountains and piedmont. There are 7 other species of *Erigeron* in the state, some of which are annuals.

April-June. (179-44-1)

ASTER

Aster curtisii Torrey & Gray

This 2-5 foot tall, profusely flowering perennial with flower heads about 1 inch across, is one of our most showy Asters. The linear to elliptic leaves are 3-6 inches long.

This southern Appalachian species, which grows in woodlands, in woodland margins, and on roadbanks in our mountain counties, is similar in many respects to *A. novi-belgii* of the coastal plain.

September-October. (179-47-25)

SILVERROD; WHITE GOLDENROD

Solidago bicolor Linnaeus

The erect stems of these perennials, with elliptic lower leaves mostly 3-4 inches long, are usually 1-3 feet tall and have only very short flowering branches.

Silverrod grows in dry, often poor soil on road banks and in open woodlands across the northern part of the state in all 3 provinces. It is native to much of the eastern U.S.

September-October. (179-49-8)

GOLDENROD

Solidago roanensis Porter

Named for Roan Mountain, where it was presumably first discovered, this Goldenrod is 1-3 feet tall and has moderately short flowering branches, giving the plant a narrow, cylindrical appearance.

These perennials grow in woodlands and along road banks only in our mountain counties; they are native to the southern Appalachians.

August-October. (179-49-10)

COMMON GOLDENROD

Solidago nemoralis Aiton

A rhizomatous perennial with pubescent stems usually 2-4 feet tall and relatively long flowering branches.

This widespread and somewhat variable species is native to the eastern U.S. and is found throughout North Carolina. It grows in old fields, pastures, waste ground, and on roadsides.

September-October. (179-49-22)

TALL GOLDENROD

Solidago altissima Linnaeus

These coarse, rhizomatous perennials, with lanceolate leaves scabrous or rough to the touch, may have stems 7 feet or more tall and an open, cone-shaped inflorescence a foot broad or high.

Native to the eastern U.S., this Goldenrod is frequent in old fields and meadows essentially throughout the state.

September-October. (179-49-30)

SLENDER-LEAVED GOLDENROD

Solidago tenuifolia Pursh

The wiry, slender stems of these perennials branch at the top to form a more or less flat cluster of flower heads. The narrow leaves, from which the plant gets its name, are 1-3 inches long.

This native of the Atlantic coast area occurs in a few of our easternmost counties where it grows in pine barrens and brackish marshes.

September-October. (179-49-37)

GREEN AND GOLD

Chrysogonum virginianum Linnaeus

Early in the season the flowering stems of these pubescent perennials are only 2-4 inches long, but later flowering stems may be 1-2 feet tall; the wide rays or "petals" of the flowering head are about ½ inch long.

A native of the central Atlantic region, *Chrysogonum* is relatively frequent in open deciduous forests of our piedmont and inner coastal plain.

March-June. (179-56-1)

WILD QUININE

Parthenium integrifolium Linnaeus

The small white flowers of this perennial are borne in compact heads that are clustered at the top of the 2-3 foot tall stems. The thick, leathery leaves, 2-3 inches long, are scurfy or rough.

Native to the central and mid-Atlantic states, these robust plants grow along the margins of deciduous woodlands and in old fields over much of the state except the high mountains and the southeast coastal plain.

June-September. (179-57-1)

OX-EYE

Heliopsis helianthoides (L.) Sweet

As the specific name implies, this perennial looks much like some of our native species of *Helianthus* or Sunflowers. The 10 or more rays or "petals," 1½ inches or more long, produce a showy "flower" 3 inches or more across.

A northeastern species that grows in woodlands, thickets, and meadows in our mountains and at scattered localities in the coastal plain.

June-October. (179-58-1)

BLACK-EYED SUSAN; CONE FLOWER

Rudbeckia hirta Linnaeus

The dark brown disc flowers in the center of the 2-3 inch flower head of these often cultivated, scabrous annuals make a colorful contrast with the bright orange-yellow ray flowers or "petals."

Native generally to the central Atlantic region and rather common in our mountains, these plants are found less frequently at scattered localities over the rest of the state. They grow on roadsides and in old fields, pastures, and meadows.

June-July. (179-61-6)

SUNFLOWER

Helianthus tomentosus Michaux

This coarse, herbaceous, rhizomatous perennial may grow 3-6 feet or more tall and the convex center or disc of the large head is about 1 inch broad. The stems are villous or hairy, and the leaves are tomentose or densely pubescent beneath.

A southeastern native that is found in woodlands and clearings chiefly in the mountains and piedmont.

June-October. (179-65-18)

NARROW-LEAVED SUNFLOWER

Helianthus angustifolius Linnaeus

The slender leaves of this tall, branched perennial are 4-8 inches long and, with the reddish purple disc flowers, help distinguish it from some of our other species of *Helianthus*.

A native of the southeastern states that is relatively frequent in marshes, wet ditches, and low meadows throughout our coastal plain and lower piedmont but rare in the mountains.

August-October. (179-65-2)

COREOPSIS

Coreopsis pubescens Elliott

These rhizomatous perennials, with opposite, usually entire leaves, are up to 3 feet or more tall. The flower heads are generally similar to those of the cultivated Coreopsis and to many of our dozen other species in this genus.

Native to the southeastern U.S., this Coreopsis grows on dry slopes and in open woods in our mountain and piedmont counties.

July-September. (179-69-7)

BUR MARIGOLD; TICK-SEED

Bidens aristosa (Michx.) Britton

These tall, profusely branched annuals produce many flower heads 2-3 inches across. The small brown fruits, each with 2 barbed teeth, stick to fur and clothing, which accounts for the common names.

One or more species of these weedy natives occur in ditches, meadows, fields, and waste places throughout the state, but *B. aristosa* is confined chiefly to the piedmont and coastal plain. *September-October.* (179-70-9)

MARSHALLIA

Marshallia graminifolia (Walt.) Small

The attractive, 1 inch broad flower heads of these 12-18 inch tall perennials are made up of only disc flowers; there are no "petals" or ray flowers.

Indigenous to the southeast, Marshallia grows in the pinelands and savannahs of our coastal plain north to the Pamlico River area where it reaches its northern limit. *July-September.* *(179-72-1)*

GAILLARDIA

Gaillardia pulchella Fougeroux

These hairy annuals, 6-24 inches tall, have wide, toothed ray flowers or "petals" ¾ inch long that are variously marked with red and yellow.

An escape from cultivation now thoroughly naturalized in about a dozen counties of our coastal plain, Gaillardia grows in sandy waste places, on roadsides, and behind beach dunes. *April-October.* *(179-74-1)*

SNEEZEWEED

Helenium autumnale Linnaeus

The stems of this perennial have a narrow wing on the angles, may be simple or branched above, and are from 1-3 feet or more tall; they bear numerous flower heads about ¾ inch across.

Essentially a species of the northeastern quarter of the U.S., these plants grow in moist pastures, meadows, and ditches more or less throughout our mountains and piedmont and less frequently in the coastal plain.

September-October. (179-75-1)

SNEEZEWEED

Helenium flexuosum Rafinesque

This plant, like the one above, has tall, wing-angled stems and small disc flowers forming a compact, globose center in the flower head. However, the smaller leaves and the brown color of the disc flowers distinguish this perennial from the other Sneezeweeds.

Native to the southeastern area of the U.S., these plants grow in moist meadows, ditches, and pastures at scattered localities over the state.

May-August. (179-75-3)

YARROW; MILFOIL

Achillea millefolium Linnaeus

The numerous small flower heads of this introduced perennial are each less than ¼ inch across, but in the aggregate form larger clusters 2-3 inches broad. The leaves, divided into many narrow segments, have a feathery appearance.

A naturalized and somewhat weedy escape from cultivation, Yarrow grows in pastures, old fields, and waste places more or less throughout the state and much of the eastern U.S. *May-October.* *(179-79-1)*

DAISY; OX-EYE DAISY

Chrysanthemum leucanthemum Linnaeus

Probably one of the few flowers known to everyone, these attractive weeds have rich yellow disc flowers and white ray flowers or "petals" that form a flower head 1½ inches or more across.

Like some other introductions, Daisies are thoroughly naturalized in fields, pastures, in waste places, and along roadsides throughout North Carolina and much of the U.S. *April-July.* *(179-82-1)*

Index

I

J

K

L

T

U

V

W

X

Y

Z